HOW TO STUDY THE BIBLE

HOW TO STUDY
THE BIBLE

Richard L. Mayhue

CHRISTIAN
FOCUS

© Richard L. Mayhue

ISBN 978-1-84550-203-4

10 9 8 7 6 5 4 3 2 1

First published in 1997 as *How to Interpret the Bible*
Reprinted 2001 as *How to Interpret the Bible for Yourself*
Reprinted in 2006 & 2009 as *How to Study the Bible*
by
Christian Focus Publications Ltd.,
Geanies House, Fearn, Ross-shire,
IV20 1TW, Great Britain

www.christianfocus.com

Cover design by Moose77.com

Printed by Norhaven A/S

Contents

TO:

Dr. Homer Kent, Jr.
Dr. Tim LaHaye
Dr. John MacArthur
Dr. Henry Morris
Dr. Charles Smith
Dr. John Sproule
Dr. Robert Thomas
Dr. John Whitcomb, Jr.
whom God has used to impress upon me
the supreme importance of *cutting it straight.*

Foreword

There are two main ways in which we all need help in approaching the Bible. The first is in our understanding of its nature and origin. That takes us immediately to such subjects as the inspiration, inerrancy, and infallibility of the Bible. But secondly we need to understand how to approach it, how to read it, how to understand its language, how to make our way through the various types of literature it contains. This is all part of the crucial biblical science of interpretation. 2 Peter 1:10 forbids us interpreting the Bible any way we like, and it is for this reason that we need principles of biblical interpretation clearly set out for us to follow. It is to this whole issue that my friend Dr. Richard Mayhue addresses himself in this excellent little book.

The book is not a heavy theological treatise addressed to academics. It is intended for all kinds of Christian people who are serious about studying the Bible carefully and interpreting it properly. He is helping us to fulfil the command we have in 2 Timothy 2:15: 'Be diligent to present yourself approved to God as a workman who does not need to be ashamed, handling accurately the word of truth.'

The contemporary Christian church greatly needs the guidance that is found in this book. It will be valuable to Christian people at all stages of their experience. The book comes from the pen of an able scholar, an experienced pastor, and a gracious Christian. I warmly commend it.

Eric Alexander

Introduction

R.A. Torrey, former president of Moody Bible Institute, offered this profound thought over a century ago: 'I learned years ago, to go to one place for the deepest lessons of life. That one place is the Bible.'

Today Christians still go to that one place, but with even greater opportunities to understand God's Word. More Bible teaching goes out faster to larger groups of people than ever before. Satellite transmissions of radio and television, the Christian publishing boom, the advent of affordable audio and video cassettes, and the computer craze has saturated our society.

However, with these unprecedented opportunities for truth comes the potential liability for error. Just because someone broadcasts a message or publishes a book does not necessarily mean that he or she is delivering God's Word as God intended it to be delivered. Thus, false teaching is abroad today more than ever.

The problem is not new. That is why Paul told Timothy, 'Be diligent to present yourself approved to God as a workman who does not need to be ashamed, handling accurately the word of truth' (2 Tim. 2:15). Without the Word being rightly divided, there would be ruined Christians (2:14) and ungodliness (2:16), and the church would be poisoned just as gangrene ravishes the human body (2:17). Hymenaeus and Philetus had gone astray in Timothy's day and had upset the faith of some with false teaching about the resurrection (2:17-18).

Our challenge is to produce a new generation of Christians who are committed to getting God's Word right; pastors and teachers who teach with meticulous care; students and parishioners who listen and learn with discernment.

How to Study the Bible is written for those who go to the Scriptures for the deepest lessons of life. It would be tragic to come to the well and drink deeply of its refreshment, only to discover that its content had been altered so that what was consumed differed from the reservoir. Likewise, it would be pitiful, having come to God's inerrant Word, to depart with an errant message.

Both scholar and new believer can be impacted by these studies. They cover a wide range of subjects and purposes including:

* Teaching a basic Bible study method
* Warning about interpretation mistakes
* Exposing current theological error
* Providing right steps to avoid wrong doctrine
* Emphasizing the truthfulness and trustworthiness of Scripture

If we understand that when we open the Scripture we handle God's Word, there will be an awesome sense of responsibility as we seek to understand what He wrote – particularly if we intend to pass it on to someone.

Years ago, as a brand new Christian, I heard Dr. Lehman Strauss tell about having 'The Word of God' stamped on the spine of his rebound Bible. That idea made a lasting impression upon me. I decided then, if my new Bible ever needed rebinding, I would do the same. Five bindings later, 'The Word of God' still graces the spine of my 'Sword' and reminds me it is not just 'a book,' rather it is 'The Book', none other than the Word of God. It demands my very best in reading, interpreting, obeying, and teaching.

God gave these words to Israel: 'But to this one I will look, to him who is humble and contrite of spirit, and who trembles at my Word' (Isa. 66:2). *How to Study the Bible* speaks to a generation of Christians who are awed by God's Word and more than anything else in life want to get it right.

I pray that our dedication to God's Word will give us the experience promised by the psalmist:

> How blessed is the man who does not walk in the counsel of the wicked,
> Nor stand in the path of sinners,
> Nor sit in the seat of scoffers!
> But his delight is in the law of the LORD,
> And in His law he meditates day and night.
> And he will be like a tree firmly planted by streams of water,
> Which yields its fruit in its season,
> And its leaf does not wither;
> And in whatever he does, he prospers (Ps. 1:1-3).

PART 1

MAKING STRAIGHT CUTS

One

Studying for God's Approval

IN LIFE there are two kinds of certainties. If you are the breadwinner in your home you might appreciate the certainty that no matter how long or how hard you shop for an item, the day after you have bought it, the article will be on sale somewhere else cheaper.

Dad, you'll remember you forgot to put the trash out front only when the garbage truck is two doors away, and you are in the shower.

For Mom there is the certainty of the chances that the bread falling with the peanut-butter-and-jelly side down are directly proportional to the cost of your carpet. Young people can identify with the certainty that it won't be until you return home from the party that you realize that you have a string of spinach stuck between your front teeth.

Earthly certainties may be humorous, but they will pass away. In reality all those things pale into insignificance when compared to the eternal certainties of God's precious Word. Our theme, *cutting it straight*, is found in 2 Timothy 2:15:

> Be diligent to present yourself approved to God as a workman who does not need to be ashamed, handling accurately the word of truth.

The *New International Version* translates it this way:

> Do your best to present yourself to God as one approved,
> a workman who does not need to be ashamed and who
> correctly handles the word of truth.

Now if we take time to read through 2 Timothy, we will
discover that when Paul handed the baton of the ministry
to Timothy, he was pre-eminently concerned with the Word
of God. He said elsewhere, 'Timothy, retain the standard of
sound words that you have heard from me' (2 Tim. 1:13). He
also wrote, 'These entrust to faithful men, who will be able
to teach others also' (2 Tim. 2:2). In 2:14, he says in effect,
'Don't stumble over words and wind up on a doctrinally
dead-end street.' He in effect warns in verses 16 and 18 of
the same chapter, 'Don't deviate doctrinally and upset the
faith of some.'

2 Timothy 3:15 says that the Word of God is the source
of the knowledge of our salvation. And in verses 16 and
17, Paul explains how that leads to growing in the grace
and the knowledge of Jesus Christ and being perfected
by God's Word. Then in 4:2 comes that great exhortation
'Preach the word.'

All of these exhortations assume and are built upon the
foundation of one particular verse – 2 Timothy 2:15. There
Paul is specifically telling Timothy that in order to minister
effectively, one must correctly interpret the Word of God.
Paul is saying, 'In order to understand what God means by
what He says, you must divide the Word of God aright.'

2 Timothy 2:15 highlights three basic ideas:

(1) the Scriptures are *impeccable*;

(2) because of that, whoever interprets the Word of God
is highly *responsible*; and

(3) our responsibility will one day be tested when we are
accountable before Almighty God for what we did with His

Word while we were here on earth. Impeccability, responsibility, and accountability.

Impeccability

The *impeccability* of Scripture is found in the last four words in both the English and Greek texts, 'The word of truth.' Paul assumes the inerrancy of Scripture here. He outlines Timothy's practical responsibilities as he comes to the Word of God in the light of the doctrine of inerrancy.

Paul asserts that Scripture is the written communication of God and that, because of that, it is consistent with the truth element of God's character. The whole doctrine of inerrancy lies upon the foundation of the character of God. If God is true (and He is), then His Word is true, and it is without error. Paul assumes that and builds upon it.

Those who like to think are probably asking, 'In what way do we equate the word of truth with the Word of God?' Psalm 31:5 says, 'O Lord God of truth.' John 17:17 says, 'Thy word is truth.' I love Psalm 119:160: 'The sum of Thy word is truth.'

So Paul reminds Timothy that his message is to be God's message. It is the Word of truth. He in effect says, 'Timothy, be careful that you don't mess it up when you handle it.' Who would change Rembrandt or Michaelangelo? If these are the lesser, then who would ever want to change the greater Word of God? We don't need to alter Scripture to bring it into harmony with truth; rather we must understand that Scripture needs to change us and the way we live so that we are brought into conformity with the Word of God.

Spurgeon once wrote that the greatest compliment ever paid to him was by one of his most antagonistic opponents. His enemy said this: 'Here is a man who has not moved an inch forward in his ministry. At the close of the nineteenth century, he's teaching the theology of the first century and is proclaiming doctrine current in Nazareth and Jerusalem in the first century.' May all of our critics be so complimentary by asserting that we have not changed the Word of God or the theology given in Scripture.

Paul in effect told Timothy, who would carry on for him, 'Timothy, the Word that you'll handle is impeccable. Just as the living Word of God was impeccable and without sin, so the written Word of God is impeccable and without error.'

Responsibility

Paul began with *impeccability*; he next told Timothy that impeccability leads to a *responsibility* on the part of the one who interprets and communicates the Word of God. I would suggest that the function of the one who interprets and communicates the Word of God is to deliver God's message as it was originally given, without deviation, whether that one is a seminary professor or pastor or Sunday school teacher or parent in the home.

This is the point that Paul was making to Timothy: 'You're handling God's Word, Timothy, not your own. Therefore be a messenger, not the originator of the message. A sower, not the source. A herald, not the authority. A steward, not the owner. A guide, not the author. A server of spiritual food, not the chef. As it was given to you straight out of the kitchen, put it on the table so people can eat it. You don't need to add to it, you do not need to rearrange it, and you do not need to take away from it.'

Faithfulness

Paul told Timothy three ways that he could measure how well he was doing with his responsibilities. The first was the test of faithfulness. He told Timothy, 'You're to be a workman.' Timothy would continually ask himself as he came to the Word of God, 'Am I really a workman? Am I at my station? Am I doing the one thing that God wants me to do and not the thousand other things that I could possibly do, or feel good in doing, or those that would be nice to do, neglecting the higher priorities that God has given me? Am I faithful to the Word that God has assigned? Am I energetically toiling at it?' That is the idea behind the Greek word for 'workman'.

These thoughts have had a profound impact on my life. I'll never come to the Word the same again. I'll never preach and teach the way I used to preach and teach. The awe-someness and the preciousness and the purity of God's Word burns deep into my heart. What an incredible responsibility it is to channel it through a human mind and out of a human mouth and then not to mess up the message.

'Timothy,' Paul said, 'your first responsibility is to be faithful to the work.' Wesley prayed for God to make him 'a man of one book'. Isn't that a great prayer? Lord, make me a man of one Book, faithful at the task of its interpretation.

Commitment

There's a second element in responsibility. Not only was Timothy to be *faithful* at the work God assigned, but he was also to be *committed*. The first word in the Greek text is the verb *spoudazō*, which means to be diligent and make haste at the task. It talks about the level of commitment that Timothy should have to the Word of God.

The King James Version says, 'Study.' If you have a *New American Standard Bible*, you will notice it says, 'Be diligent.' I like the *New International Version* at this point, for it says,

'Do your best.' That means to operate, function, and be involved at the very highest level of commitment and excellence because the Word of truth demands nothing less than our very best. In God's sight nothing else is acceptable.

Today there are at least four basic attacks on our commitment to the Scripture. Number one is the *higher critical* attack, which is the attack by which everything in the Bible is questioned. The Word of God is submitted to the mind of man rather than the other way around.

Then there is the *cultic* attack; men subtract or add to Scripture. There is also the *cultural* attack; Scripture is interpreted through the grip of some modern academic discipline like science, psychology, history, or the current culture.

But I think the fourth attack on the Scripture is far worse than any of these three. Worse than the higher critical, worse than the cultic, and worse than the cultural is the *hypocritical* attack, where one believes and preaches and fights for inerrancy but then treats the Word of God in a shoddy, slipshod, inadequate, halfway manner.

God is looking for the kind of person about whom Isaiah 66:2 speaks: 'But to this one I will look. To him who is humble and contrite of spirit, and who trembles at My word.' He is looking for someone who comes to the Word of God knowing that in fact he is standing before God Himself and trembling at the Word of God because it stands in judgement over him. God is looking for a man like Ezra, who said it was his goal to study the law and practise it and teach it (Ezra 7:10).

Let me add a practical note to all of this. There are two kinds of commitment required in order for us to do all that God wants. One is the commitment to study. But beyond that, those of you who perhaps have not been called to full-time ministry on a church staff have a greater commitment as a part of the flock fed by the pastor. That is the commitment to allow him to study, to encourage him to study, and in some cases even to insist that he study, that he get the Word of God right, and that he not feed you a 'junk food' meal (or, even worse, poison you by the things that he preaches and teaches).

Paul said Timothy was to be faithful. Second, he was to be committed, operating at his highest level of excellence.

Skill

Third, Timothy was to be skillful in carrying out his work at a higher and higher level as he grew in handling the Word of God. That might be hard to understand at first. *Faithfulness* and *commitment* seem to be enough, but I would suggest to you that one more step is necessary: to bring the skilled discipline of interpreting the Word of God to the text in order to do what Paul says – handle it accurately.

There must be no deviation or falsification. Strong warnings are given against changing or perverting or mutilating or distorting or adding to or to taking away.

The English phrase 'handling accurately' is actually one word in the Greek text – *orthotomeō*. It is used in Greek literature when talking of a guide's 'cutting a straight path'; or when referring to a priest who was to slice the animal just right according to God's instructions; or a farmer cutting a straight furrow; or of a builder cutting the rocks just right to place them in a decorative and pleasing arrangement in the building. It was used also of a tailor or tentmaker's cutting cloth or of a husband who cut the bread right as he fed his family.

But here a pastor is to cut the Word of God straight, giving it out just as God gave it. What Paul is demanding of Timothy at this point is faultless workmanship. The prayer of anyone who undertakes to teach the Word of God ought to be, 'Lord, help me to get it right.'

I want to keep our thoughts in the same vein that Paul intended for Timothy. Paul's counsel was really a reminder and a warning to Timothy. I hope none of us have been Christians so long that we have grown so complacent or proud that we don't realize we need to be reminded. The New Testament is full of reminders. Day by day we need to be warned so that we never slip away from that cutting edge of excellence.

Accountability

It is imperative to remember that one day all of us who have ever handled the Word of God will stand *accountable* to God Himself for our interpretation, our teaching, and our messages. The text says that there will be a test; the Greek word is **dokizamō**, which means testing with the desire to approve. The text also says that we will stand before God, not before church leaders, not before governments, and not before seminary professors.

Paul put it best in 1 Corinthians 4:4 when in response to the challenge of that church he says, 'The one who examines me is the Lord.' I like the way J.B. Phillips paraphrases 2 Timothy 2:15, 'Concentrate on winning God's approval.' Not just upon getting a lesson, not just upon getting a sermon, not upon hearing people say, 'Amen,' not upon getting notes from your people saying, 'Pastor, that was great,' but 'concentrate on winning God's approval.'

If we really took this text to heart, along with James 3:1, not so many of us would want to be teachers. James put it this way: 'Let not many of you become teachers, my brethren, knowing that as such we shall incur a stricter judgement.' There is accountability. The thought is this: any time you ever teach or preach, there ought to be one primary thought in your mind, *God is the ultimate audience.* When preparing and writing and thinking, our souls ought to be stirred by the urgency for excellence because God is the one who will ultimately judge our message.

There will be a test; we are going to stand before God. Not only will there will be a test, but the Scripture indicates that there can be a 'trauma.' Why? Because we will stand there before God, and the only issue that is in question is whether we will 'stand ashamed' or whether we will 'stand approved by Him'. The logical conclusion for those who have been unfaithful (not keeping at the work) and those who have been uncommitted (operating at less than their best) and those that have been operating unskilled (producing sloppy work) is shame before God. That is traumatic.

Wouldn't it be horrible to one day stand in disgrace before God because we didn't handle aright His Word? But Paul says if we get it right, if we don't mess it up, and if we cut it straight, there will be God's approval. Approved workmen are not ashamed. If we faithfully deliver the truth as He has given it to us in His Word, then we shall receive the word that all of us want to hear, 'Well done, My good and faithful servant.'

So goes the message of 2 Timothy 2:15. It speaks of a Word that's *impeccable*, faultless, without error, which demands a responsible interpretation for which God will one day hold us *accountable*.

The following chapters are designed to make us better workmen and to equip us to stand approved. Some deal with developing the necessary skills of Bible study and others focus on contemporary errors to avoid. The next chapter answers the strategically important question: 'How did we get our Bible?'

Questions for Discussion
1. What does the doctrine of the inerrancy of Scripture mean?

2. In what three ways may we measure how well we handle our responsibility to accurately interpret Scripture?

3. Read 2 Timothy 2:15. What does commitment to Scripture mean? How do we know whether or not our commitment is high?

4. Describe the four basic attacks against our commitment to the Word of God. Why are they dangerous?

5. What does the phrase *handling accurately* describe?

6. In what way are we being held accountable for our interpretation of Scripture?

Two

How Did We Get Our Bible?

Hailed as the twentieth century's 'prince of expositors', G. Campbell Morgan was a messenger widely used by God. However, he wrestled with the integrity of Scripture early in his life. He concluded that if there were errors in the biblical message, it could not be honestly proclaimed in public as God's holy, inerrant Word. Here is the account of how young Campbell Morgan finally concluded that the Bible was surely God's Word.

At last the crisis came when he admitted to himself his total lack of assurance that the Bible was the authoritative Word of God to man. He immediately cancelled all preaching engagements. Then, taking all his books, both those attacking and defending the Bible, he put them all in a corner cupboard. Relating this afterwards, as he did many times in preaching, he told of turning the key in the lock of the door. 'I can hear the click of that lock now,' he used to say. He went out of the house, and down the street to a bookshop. He bought a new Bible and, returning to his room with it, he said to himself: 'I am no longer sure that this is what my father claims it to be – the Word of God. But of this I am sure. If it be the Word of God, and if I come to it with an unprejudiced and open mind, it will bring assurance to my soul of itself.' 'That Bible found me,' he said, 'I began to read and study it then, in 1883. I have been a student ever since, and I still am (in 1938).'[1]

Has God Said?

Ever since Eve encountered Satan's barrage of doubt and denial (Gen. 3:1-7), mankind has continued to question God's Word. Unfortunately, Eve had little or no help in sorting through her intellectual obstacles to full faith in God's self-disclosure (Gen. 2:16-17).

Now the Scripture certainly has more than enough content to be interrogated, considering that it's comprised of sixty-six books, 1,189 chapters, 31,173 verses, and 774,746 words. When you open your English translation to read or study, you might have asked in the past or are currently asking, as did G. Campbell Morgan, 'How can I be sure this is the unadulterated Word of God?'

Questions of this kind are not altogether bad, especially when we seek to learn with a teachable mind (Acts 17:11). The Scripture invites the kinds of queries that a sincere student asks. A whole host of questions can flood the mind, such as:

- Where did the Bible come from?
- Whose thinking does it reflect?
- Did any books of the Bible get lost in time past?
- What does the Scripture claim for itself?
- Does it live up to its claims?
- Who wrote the Bible – God or man?
- Has Scripture been protected from human tampering over the centuries?
- How close to the original manuscripts are today's translations?
- How did the Bible get to our time and language?
- Is there more Scripture to come, beyond the current sixty-six books?

- Who determined and on what basis that the Bible would be composed of the traditional list of sixty six books?
- If the Scriptures were written over a period of 1,500 years (*ca.* 1405 BC to AD 95), passed down since then for almost 2,000 years, and translated into several thousand languages, what prevented the Bible from being changed by the carelessness or ill motives of men?
- Does today's Bible really deserve the title 'The Word of God'?

Undoubtedly, some of these questions bombarded the mind of Campbell Morgan which caused the anchor of his faith in Scripture to slip. A study of the Scriptures alone settled all his questions to the extent that he was never bothered by them again. In this brief chapter, we want to let the sacred text of Scripture give us the same assurance too.

Scripture's Self Claims

Like Morgan did, we take the Bible and let it speak for itself. Does it claim to be God's Word? Over 2,000 times in the Old Testament alone, the Bible asserts that God spoke what is written within. From the beginning (Gen. 1:3) to the end (Mal. 4:3) and continually throughout, this is what Scripture claims.

The phrase 'the Word of God' occurs over forty times in the New Testament. It is equated with the Old Testament (Mark 7:13). It is what Jesus preached (Luke 5:1). It was the message the apostles taught (Acts 4:31 and 6:2). It was the word the Samaritans received (Acts 8:14) as given by the apostles (Acts 8:25). It was the message the Gentiles received as preached by Peter (Acts 11:1). It was the word

Paul preached on his first missionary journey (Acts 13:5, 7, 44, 48, 49; 15:35-36). It was the message preached on Paul's second missionary journey (Acts 16:32; 17:13; 18:11). It was the message Paul preached on his third missionary journey (Acts 19:10). It was the focus of Luke in the Book of Acts in that it spread rapidly and widely (Acts 6:7; 12:24; 19:20). Paul was careful to tell the Corinthians that he spoke the Word as it was given from God, that it had not been adulterated, and that it was a manifestation of truth (2 Cor. 2:17; 4:2). Paul acknowledged that it was the source of his preaching (Col. 1:25; 1 Thess. 2:13).

Psalms 19 and 119 plus Proverbs 30:5-6 make powerful statements about God's Word which sets it apart from any other religious instruction ever known in the history of mankind. These passages make the case for the Bible being called 'sacred' (2 Tim. 3:15) and 'holy' (Rom. 1:2).

The Bible claims ultimate spiritual authority in doctrine, reproof, correction, and instruction in righteousness because it represents the will of Almighty God (2 Tim. 3:16-17). Scripture asserts its spiritual sufficiency, so much so that it claims exclusivity for its teaching (cf. Isa. 55:11; 2 Pet. 1:3-4).

God's Word declares that it is *inerrant* (Pss. 12:6, 119:140; Prov. 30:5a; John 10:35) and *infallible* (2 Tim. 3:16-17). In other words, it is true and therefore trustworthy. All of these qualities are dependent on the fact that the Scriptures are *inspired* of God (2 Tim. 3:16; 2 Pet. 1:20-21) which guarantees its quality at the Source and at its first written record.

In Scripture, the person of God and the Word of God are everywhere interrelated. So much so, that whatever is true about the character of God is true about the nature of God's Word. God is true, impeccable, and reliable; therefore, so is His Word. What a person thinks about God's Word, in reality, reflects what a person thinks about God.

Thus, the Scripture can make these demands on its readers.

> And He humbled you and let you be hungry, and fed you with manna which you did not know, nor did your fathers know, that He might make you understand that man does not live by bread alone, but man lives by everything that proceeds out of the mouth of the LORD (Deut. 8:3).

> I have not departed from the command of His lips; I have treasured the words of His mouth more than my necessary food (Job 23:12).

The Publishing Process

The Bible does not expect its reader to speculate on how these divine qualities were transferred from God to His Word, but rather anticipates the questions with convincing answers. Every generation of skeptics has assailed the self-claims of the Bible, but its own explanations and answers have been more than equal to the challenge. The Bible has gone through God's editorial process in being given to and distributed among the human race. Its several features are discussed below.

Revelation

God took the initiative to disclose or reveal Himself to mankind (Heb. 1:1). The vehicles varied; sometimes it was through the created order, at other times through visions/ dreams or speaking prophets. However, the most complete and understandable self-disclosures were through the propositions of Scripture (1 Cor. 2:6-16). The revealed Word of God is unique in that it is the only revelation of God that is so complete and so clearly declares man's sinfulness and God's provision of the Saviour.

Inspiration
The written revelation of God, the Scriptures, are also characterized by the 'inspiration' quality. This has more to do with the process by which God revealed Himself than the fact of His self-revelation. 'All Scripture is inspired by God ...' (2 Tim 3:16) makes the claim. Peter explains the process: 'But know this first of all, that no prophecy of Scripture is *a matter* of one's own interpretation, for no prophecy was ever made by an act of human will, but men moved by the Holy Spirit spoke from God' (2 Pet. 1:20-21). By this means, the Word of God is protected from human error in its original record by the ministry of the Holy Spirit (*cf.* Deut. 18:18; Matt. 1:22). Zechariah 7:12 describes it most clearly:

> And they made their hearts like flint so that they could not hear the law and the words which the Lord of hosts had sent by His Spirit through the former prophets; therefore great wrath came from the Lord of hosts.

This ministry of the Spirit extends to both the parts (the words) and to the whole in the autographa, i.e. the original writings.

Canonicity
We must understand that from one perspective the Bible is actually one book with one Divine Author. On the other hand, it was written over a period of fifteen hundred years through the pens of almost forty human authors. The Bible began with the creation account of Genesis 1-2, written by Moses about 1405 bc, and extends to the eternity future account of Revelation 21-22, written by the Apostle John

about AD 95. During this time, God progressively revealed Himself and His purposes in the inspired Scriptures. But this raises a significant question: 'How do we know what supposed sacred writings were to be included in the canon of Scripture and which ones were to be excluded?'

Over the centuries, three widely recognized principles were used to validate those writings which came as a result of Divine revelation and inspiration. First, the writing had to have a recognized prophet or apostle as its author. Second, the writing could not disagree with or contradict previous Scripture. Third, the writing had to have wide acceptance by the community of believers. Thus, when various church councils met to consider the canon, they did not decide the canonicity of a book but rather recognized, after the fact, what God had already accomplished.

With regard to the Old Testament, by the time of Christ all of the Old Testament had been written and accepted in the Jewish community. The last book, Malachi, had been completed about 430 BC. Not only did the Old Testament canon of Christ's day conform to the Old Testament which has since been used throughout the centuries, but it did not contain the Apocrypha. This was a group of fourteen rogue writings which were written after Malachi and attached to the Old Testament about 200–150 BC in the Greek translation of the Hebrew Old Testament called the Septuagint (LXX), thus appearing to this very day in some versions of the Bible. However, not one writing from the Apocrypha is cited by a New Testament writer nor did Jesus affirm any of them as He did the recognized Old Testament canon of His era (cf. Luke 24:27, 44).

By Christ's time, the Old Testament canon had been divided up into two lists of 22 or 24 books respectively, each of which contained the same material as the thirty-nine books of our modern versions. In the twenty-two book canon, Jeremiah and Lamentations were considered as one, as were Judges and Ruth. Here is how the twenty-four book format was divided.

THE HEBREW OLD TESTAMENT

LAW
1. Genesis
2. Exodus
3. Leviticus
4. Numbers
5. Deuteronomy

PROPHETS
A. Former Prophets
   6. Joshua
   7. Judges
   8. Samuel
   9. Kings

B. *Latter Prophets*
   10. Isaiah
   11. Jeremiah
   12. Ezekiel
   13. The Twelve

WRITINGS
A. *Poetical Books*
   14. Psalms
   15. Proverbs
   16. Job

B. *Five Rolls*
   (Megilloth)
   17. Song of Songs
   18. Ruth
   19. Lamentations
   20. Ecclesiastes
   21. Esther

C. *Historical Books*
   22. Daniel
   23. Ezra-Nehemiah
   24. Chronicles

The same three key tests applied to the New Testament. In the case of Mark and Luke/Acts, they were considered to be, in effect, the penmen for Peter and Paul respectively. James and Jude were written by Christ's half-brothers. While Hebrews is the only New Testament book whose authorship is unknown for certain, its content is so in line with both the Old Testament and New Testament, that the early church concluded it must have been written by an apostolic associate. The twenty-seven books of the modern New Testament have been generally accepted since *ca.* AD 350–400.

Preservation
How can we be sure that the revealed and inspired, written Word of God, which was recognized as canonical by the early church, has been handed down to our times without any loss of material?

Furthermore, have the Scriptures survived Satan's destructive onslaught? One of the devil's prime concerns in life is to undermine the Bible. In the beginning, he denied God's Word to Eve (Gen. 3:4). Satan later attempted to distort the Scripture in his wilderness encounter with Christ (Matt. 4:6-7). Through King Jehoiakim, he even attempted to literally destroy the Word (Jer. 36:23). The battle for the Bible rages, but Scripture has and will continue to outlast its enemies.

God anticipated man's and Satan's malice towards the Scripture with Divine promises to preserve His Word. The very continued existence of Scripture is guaranteed in Isaiah 40:8 (cf. 1 Pet. 1:25).

> The grass withers, the flower fades, but the word of our God stands forever.

This even means that no inspired Scripture has been lost in the past and now awaits rediscovery.

The actual content of Scripture will be perpetuated, both in heaven (Ps. 119:89) and on earth (Isa. 59:21). Thus the purposes of God, as published in the sacred writings, will never be thwarted, even in the least detail (cf. Matt. 5:18, 24:35; Mark 13:3; Luke 16:17).

> So shall My word be which goes forth from My mouth; it shall not return to Me empty, without accomplishing what I desire, and without succeeding *in the matter* for which I sent it (Isa. 55:11).

Transmission

Since the Bible has frequently been translated into multiple languages and distributed throughout the world, how can we be sure that error has not crept in, even if it was unintentional? As Christianity spread, it is certainly true that people desired to have the Bible in their own language which required translations from the original Hebrew and Aramaic languages of the Old Testament and the Greek of the New Testament. Not only did translators provide an opportunity for error but publication, which was done by hand copying until the printing press arrived about 1450, also afforded continual possibilities of error.

The practitioners of textual criticism, a precise science, have discovered, preserved, catalogued, evaluated, and published an amazing array of biblical manuscripts from both the Old and New Testaments. In fact, the number of existing biblical manuscripts dramatically outdistances the extant fragments of any other ancient literature. By comparing text with text, the textual critic can confidently determine what the original prophetic/apostolic, inspired writing contained.

Although existing copies of the chief, ancient Hebrew text (Massoretic) date back only to the tenth century AD, two other important lines of textual evidence bolster the confidence of textual critics that they have reclaimed the autographa. First, the tenth century AD Hebrew Old Testament can be compared to the Greek translation called the Septuagint or LXX (written *ca.* 200-150 BC; the oldest extant manuscript dates to *ca.* AD 325). There is an amazing parallel between the two which speaks of the accuracy in copying the Hebrew text for centuries. Second, the discovery of the Dead Sea Scrolls in 1947-1956 (manuscripts that are dated *ca.* 200-100 BC) proved to be monumentally important. After comparing the earlier Hebrew texts with the later ones, only a few slight variants were discovered, none of which changed the meaning of any passage. Although the Old Testament had been translated and copied for centuries, the latest version was essentially the same as the earlier ones.

The New Testament findings are even more decisive because a much larger amount of material is available for study; there are over 5,000 Greek New Testament manuscripts that range from whole Bibles to scraps of papyri which contain as little as one partial verse. A few existing fragments date to within twenty-five to fifty years of the original writing. New Testament textual critics have generally concluded that (1) 99.99 percent of the original writings have been reclaimed and (2) of the remaining one hundredth of one percent, there are no variants substantially affecting any Christian doctrine.

With this wealth of biblical manuscripts in the original languages and with the disciplined ability of textual critics to establish with almost perfect accuracy the content of the autographa, then any errors which have been introduced and/or perpetuated by the thousands of translations over the centuries can be identified and corrected by comparing the translation or copy with the reassembled original. By this providential means, God has made good His promise to preserve the Scriptures. We can rest assured that there are translations available today which indeed are worthy of the title, The Word of God.

The history of a full, English translation Bible essentially begins with John Wycliffe (*ca.* 1330-1384) who made the first English translation of the whole Bible. Later, William Tyndale is associated with the first complete, printed New Testament in English (*ca.* 1526). Myles Coverdale followed in 1535 by delivering the first complete Bible printed in English. By 1611, the *King James Version* (KJV) had been completed. Since then, hundreds of translations have been made – some better, some worse. Today, the better to best English translations of the Hebrew and Greek Scriptures include: (1) *New King James Version* (NKJV); (2) *English Standard Version* (ESV); and (3) *New American Standard Bible* (NASB).

Summing It Up

God intended His Word to abide forever (preservation). Therefore His written, propositional, self disclosure (revelation) was protected from error in its original writing (inspiration) and collected in sixty-six books of the Old and New Testaments (canonicity).

Through the centuries, tens of thousands of copies and thousands of translations have been made (transmission) which did introduce error. Because there is an abundance of existing ancient Old Testament and New Testament manuscripts, however, the exacting science of textual criticism has been able to reclaim the content of the original writings (revelation and inspiration) to the extreme degree of 99.99 percent, with the remaining one hundredth of one per cent having no effect on its content (preservation).

The sacred book which we read, study, obey, and preach deserves to unreservedly be called The Bible or 'The Book without peer' since its author is God and it bears the qualities of (1) total truth and (2) complete trustworthiness that also characterize its Divine source.

Is There More To Come?

How do we know that God will not amend our current Bible with a 67th inspired book? Or in other words, 'Is the canon forever closed?'

Three Old Testament texts warn that no one should delete from or add to Scripture (Deut. 4:2; 12:32; Prov. 30:6). Realizing that additional canonical books actually came after these words of warning, we can only conclude that while no deletions whatsoever were authorized, in fact, authorized, inspired writings were permitted to be added. These texts, then, do not prohibit more Scripture and thus do not settle the issue.

However, these same thoughts are found later in the final book of the Scriptural canon which has been closed now for 1,900 years.

> I testify to everyone who hears the words of the prophecy of this book: if anyone adds to them, God shall add to him the plagues which are written in this book; and if anyone takes away from the words of the book of this prophecy, God shall take away his part from the tree of life and from the holy city, which are written in this book (Rev. 22:18-19).

Several significant observations, when taken together, have convinced the church over the centuries that the canon of Scripture is actually closed, never to be reopened.

(1) The book of Revelation is unique to the Scripture in that it describes with unparalleled detail the end-times events which precede eternity future. As Genesis began Scripture by bridging the gap from eternity past into our time/space existence with the only detailed creation account (Gen. 1-2), so Revelation transitions out of time/space back into eternity future (Rev. 20-22). Genesis and Revelation, by their contents, are the perfectly matched bookends of Scripture, i.e. the 'Alpha and Omega' of the canon, the beginning and the end.

(2) Just as there was prophetic silence after Malachi completed the Old Testament canon, so there was a parallel

silence after John delivered Revelation. This leads to the conclusion that the New Testament canon was then closed also.

(3) Since there have not been nor now are any authorized prophets or apostles in the Old Testament and New Testament sense, then there are no potential authors of future inspired, canonical writings.

(4) Of the four exhortations not to tamper with Scripture, only the one in Revelation 22:18-19 contains warnings of severe Divine judgment for disobedience. Further, Revelation is the only book of the New Testament to end with this kind of admonition. Therefore, these facts strongly suggest that (a) Revelation was the last book of the canon and (b) now that the Book is complete, to either add or delete would bring God's severe displeasure.

(5) Finally, the early church, those closest in time to the Apostles, believed that Revelation concluded God's inspired writings, the Scriptures.

So we can conclude, based on solid Biblical reasoning, that the canon is and will remain closed. There will be no future 67th book of the Bible.

Where Do We Stand?

In April 1521, Martin Luther appeared before his ecclesiastical accusers at the Diet of Worms. They had given him the ultimatum to repudiate his unwavering faith in the sufficiency and perspicuity of the Scriptures. Luther is said to have responded, 'Unless I am convicted by Scripture and plain reason – I do not accept the authority of popes and councils, for they have contradicted each other – my conscience is captive to the Word of God .... God help me! Here I stand.'[2]

Like G. Campbell Morgan and Martin Luther, may we rise above the doubts within and confront the threats without when God's Word is assailed. God, help us to be loyal contenders for the faith which was once for all delivered to the saints (Jude 3). Let us stand with God and the Scripture alone. Lord, assist us to 'cut Your Word straight!'

And for this reason we also constantly thank God that when you received from us the word of God's message, you accepted it not as the word of men, but for what it really is, the word of God, which also performs its work in you who believe (1 Thess. 2:13).

Questions for Discussion

1. Look up the indicated verses and discover how the Word of God works in believers (1 Thess. 2:13).

a.	_____	us	(1 Pet. 1:23)
b.	_____	us	(2 Tim. 3:16)
c.	_____	us	(2 Tim. 3:16)
d.	_____	us	(2 Tim. 3:16)
e.	_____	us	(2 Tim. 3:16)
f.	_____	us	(2 Tim. 3:17)
g.	_____	us	(Ps. 119:105)
h.	_____	us	(Ps. 119:24)
i.	_____	us	(Ps. 119:154)
j.	_____	us	(Ps. 19:7)
k.	_____	us	(Ps. 19:11)
l.	_____	us	(1 Pet. 2:2)
m.	_____	us	(Heb. 4:12)
n.	_____	us	(John 17:17)

o. _____ us   (John 8:31-32)
p. _____ us   (Col. 3:16)
q. _____ us   (Ps. 119:11)
r. _____ us   (Ps. 119:28)
s. _____ us   (Ps. 19:8)
t. Makes us   (Ps. 119:97-100)

2. Because God's Word is so fresh and powerful (Ps. 119:89-90; Isa. 55:8-11), what should you do to insure that you benefit from it? Job 23:12 and James 1:22 will help to compose your answer.

Three

Tools for Cutting It Straight

THE FAMOUS American evangelist Billy Sunday once described reading the Bible as an experience similar to travelling.

I entered through the portico of Genesis and walked down through the Old Testament art gallery where the pictures of Abraham, Moses, Joseph, Isaiah, David and Solomon hung on the walls.

I passed into the music room of the Psalms and every reed of God's great organ responded to the tuneful harp of David.

I entered the chamber of Ecclesiastes where the voice of the preacher was heard, and into the conservatory of Sharon and the lily of the valley's spices filled and perfumed my life.

I entered the business office of the Proverbs, then into the observation room of the prophets where I saw telescopes of various sizes, some pointing to far-off events but all concentrated upon the bright star which was to rise above the moonlit hills of Judea for our salvation.

I entered the audience room of the King of Kings and passed into the correspondence rooms where sat Matthew, Mark, Luke, John, Paul, Peter and James penning their epistles.

I stepped then into the throne room of Revelation and caught a vision of the King sitting on His throne in all His glory, and I cried:

> All hail the power of Jesus' name,
> Let angels prostrate fall,
> Bring forth the royal diadem,
> And crown Him Lord of all.

There are two ways to take the biblical journey; either through the experience of another person like Billy Sunday or by personally learning to interpret (walk through) the Bible yourself. It is this latter intimate involvement that will make trips through the pages of Scripture unforgettable.

Interpreting the Bible takes you along the pathways of history. You walk where you have never been before, at times in real danger of losing your way or even crashing over the side. On other occasions people will even depend on you to keep them on the trail.

While seeking a firsthand experience, you will still need seasoned guides who have gone this way before. They can lead through new territory, over troublesome terrain, and around dangerous obstacles. They also will serve to keep you from getting lost or ending up on a dead-end path. Beyond this, they will point out important details that might be overlooked in your beginning travels.

Books serve as these invaluable guides to traverse the way of God's Word. They enable you to 'walk' it straight for yourself.

Which Bible?
We start with 'The Book' – the Bible. Hebrew, Aramaic, and Greek constituted the original languages of Scripture. Since most of us don't use these ancient languages today, the foremost guide we seek is a good English translation of the Bible.

The key question for any Christian to ask and answer is, 'Which translation of the Bible should I use for my personal study?'

There are three translations that I recommend. Each is a little different, but all are sound. You will want to choose the Bible with which you feel most comfortable. Look for a Bible that is enjoyable to read and lends itself to ease of understanding.

My three choices include the *English Standard Version* (ESV), the *New American Standard Bible* (NASB), or the *King James Version* (KJV); (also its updated equivalent, the *New King James Version*). Many of you are already familiar with one of these versions and should stick with it. Others still search for just the right translation.

For those of you who are still hunting, let me show you a sample passage from each translation. Your decision will be made easier by comparing identical passages from different Bibles. Look at three renderings of Ephesians 4:11-16 on the following page.

After choosing a translation, stick with it. Make that Bible your constant companion for reading, studying, memorizing, and following along in church or the classroom. It thus becomes your own personal Bible.

Often people ask about paraphrases and how they differ from translations. Two of the best are *The Living Bible* and *The New Testament in Modern English.*

Kenneth Taylor and J.B. Phillips were not attempting so much to translate the Bible from the original languages into English as they were to put the English translation into an expanded, interpretative form for ease of understanding. If you read the forewords to both, you will appreciate what these gentlemen set out to accomplish.

ESV	NASB	KJV
And he gave the apostles, the prophets, the evangelists, the pastors and teachers, to equip the saints for the work of ministry, for building up the body of Christ, until we all attain to the unity of the faith and of the knowledge of the Son of God, to mature manhood, to the measure of the stature of the fullness of Christ, so that we may no longer be children, tossed to and fro by the waves and carried about by every wind of doctrine, by human cunning, by craftiness in deceitful schemes. Rather, speaking the truth in love, we are to grow up in every way into him who is the head, into Christ, from whom the whole body, joined and held together by every joint with which it is equipped, when each part is working properly, makes the body grow so that it builds itself up in love.	And He gave some as apostles, and some as prophets and some as evangelists, and some as pastors and teachers, for the equipping of the saints for the work of service, to the building up of the body of Christ; until we all attain to the unity of the faith, and of the knowledge of the Son of God, to a mature man, to the measure of the stature which belongs to the fulness of Christ. As a result, we are no longer to be children, tossed here and there by waves, and carried about by every wind of doctrine, by the trickery of men, by craftiness in deceitful scheming; but speaking the truth in love, we are to grow up in all aspects into Him, who is the head, even Christ, from whom the whole body, being fitted and held together by that which every joint supplies, according to the proper working of each individual part, cause the growth of the body for the building up of itself in love.	And he gave some, apostles; and some, prophets; and some, evangelists; and some, pastors and teachers; for the perfecting of the saints, for the work of the ministry, for the edifying of the body of Christ: till we all come in the unity of faith, and of the knowledge of the Son of God, unto a perfect man, unto the measure of the stature of the fulness of Christ: that we henceforth be no more children, tossed to and fro, and carried about with every wind of doctrine, by the sleight of men, and cunning craftiness, whereby they lie in wait to deceive; but speaking the truth in love, may grow up into him in all things, which is the head, even Christ: from whom the whole body fitly joined together and compacted by that which every joint supplieth, according to the effectual working in the measure of every part, maketh increase of the body unto the edifying of itself in love.

A paraphrase should be used as a commentary (an interpretation of the text) rather than as a study Bible (a translation of the text). To use a paraphrase as a study Bible is to bypass the most important step – i.e. you having the opportunity to interpret the Bible for yourself.

One last question is, 'What reference Bibles are available and reliable?' There are three that I recommend:

* *MacArthur Study Bible*, Thomas Nelson
* *NIV Study Bible*, Zondervan
* *Thompson Chain Reference Bible*, Kirkbride

If you are still looking, why not find several friends who have all of the options. For a short time borrow the various Bibles so you can compare them all at once. Then choose the Bible that is best for you, and you will be ready to expand your library.

Which set of books?

I can vividly remember as a new Christian being motivated to study the Bible by my pastor, Tim La Haye. He recommended that Christians study the Bible with some basic tools.

So I rushed down to the Bible bookstore in La Mesa, California, to buy my first books. They included a Bible atlas, a Bible dictionary, and a standard commentary set.

Since then I have added hundreds of volumes to my library. Yet in my own personal study, I find myself most frequently using some of the first books I bought because they are the real work horses of interpreting Scripture.

I am frequently asked, 'If you were starting a library, what books would you purchase?' The answer really depends on how serious a person is about studying and how much money is available to invest.

For someone just starting out, I recommend a 'starter set' containing a basic minimum of tools for cutting it straight. This set includes:

* Bible atlas
* Bible dictionary
* English concordance
* Bible commentary
* Theology volumes

As more money becomes available or your interest in the Bible grows, you can expand into the 'student's set.' It is also possible that some would want to start at this level. This set includes the sort of books in the 'starter set' along with these additional volumes:

* Topical Bible
* Bible encyclopaedia
* Bible backgrounds
* Old Testament word helps
* New Testament word helps

For those of you who want to take your study seriously and use your discoveries beyond a personal level, I recommend the 'speaker's set'. Most will want to grow into this set, having begun at the starter or student level.

In addition to the volumes recommended for the two previous sets, I would add:

* Greek helps
* English-Greek concordance
* Figure of speech helps
* Ethics volume
* Cross-reference helps

Which specific books?

The next logical question is, Which specific books in each category will guide me best? I want to recommend some individual books that have proved to be faithful guides and dependable tools for me in studying Scripture. For your help I mention the publishers of the editions I possess, but it is possible that the books I list are available from other publishers, depending on the country in which you live.

Bible atlas

* Barry Beitzel, *Moody Atlas of Bible Lands*, Moody (Starter and Seeker)
* Yohanan Aharoni and Michael Avi-Yonah, *The MacMillan Bible Atlas*, MacMillan (Speaker)

You will find a Bible atlas invaluable when studying the Old Testament historical books, the Gospels, and Acts. These books will come alive when you can reconstruct the route of Paul's missionary journeys, trace the path of the Exodus, or follow the flow of Christ's life.

You will be able to map out all the battles fought in Joshua or travel with David as he flees from Saul. If you ever wondered why Christ chose seven specific churches of Revelation 2-3 to receive His letters, one look at a Bible atlas will satisfy your curiosity.

Bible dictionary

* *Unger's Bible Dictionary*, Moody (Starter)
* *The New Bible Dictionary*, Eerdmans (Student and Speaker)

A Bible dictionary serves as a quick source of a wide variety of information presented in comprehensive style. The widow and her mite of Luke 21 will be more meaningful when you look up 'mite', or the whole Tabernacle experience of Exodus and Numbers will be more understandable by reading an overview of the 'Tabernacle.'

You can learn about 'Pontius Pilate' or get some good background about the 'feasts and festivals' found in Leviticus and the Gospels. If you have ever wondered about the 'Bema,' or 'judgement seat,' in 1 Corinthians 3 and 2 Corinthians 5, a Bible dictionary will help you understand.

English concordance

* *Young's Analytical Concordance* (KJV)
* *Strong's Exhaustive Concordance* (KJV)
* *New American Standard Exhaustive Concordance of the Bible*
* NIV *Complete Concordance*

A concordance lists each English word used in a particular translation. It is invaluable for quickly tracing what the Bible says about a person, a place, a word, or a theme. Also when you are frustrated because you can remember a verse but not its location, the concordance will help you locate this verse.

Bible commentary

* J. Sidlow Baxter, *Explore the Book*, Zondervan (Starter)
* *Everyman's Bible Commentary* series, Moody (Student)

* *The Bible Knowledge Commentary* (OT and NT), Victor (Student)
* *The Expositor's Bible Commentary* series, Zondervan (Speaker)
* *Focus on the Bible* series, Christian Focus (Starter and Student)

Commentaries are essentially 'comments' or interpretations of the biblical text. They are most helpful where a passage is not self-explanatory. They are a must for studying books like Ecclesiastes or Revelation. Those tough passages like Acts 2 or Isaiah 53 become easier to understand when a master teacher guides you through with his commentary.

Theology volumes

* Stephen Swihart, *The Victor Bible Source Book*, Victor (Starter)
* William Evans, *The Great Doctrines of the Bible*, Moody (Starter and Seeker)
* John Walvoord and Lewis S. Chafer, *Major Bible Themes*, Zondervan (Student)
* Emory Bancroft, *Christian Theology*, Zondervan (Speaker)
* Henry Thiessen, *Lectures in Systematic Theology*, Eerdmans (Speaker)

All that the Bible says about a subject or doctrine is usually not confined to just one passage. A theology volume will provide thorough biblical background for the subject you are dealing with.

For example, it will shed light on the humanity and deity of Jesus Christ, the ministry of the Holy Spirit in the Old and New Testaments, the trinity of God, salvation, prophecy, and a host of other doctrinal matters. A theology volume allows you to see the facet you are studying in light of all the rest that the Bible teaches on the subject.

Topical Bible

* *Nave's Topical Bible*, Moody (Student)
* Harold Monser, *Topical Index and Digest of the Bible*, Baker (Speaker)
* *MacArthur Topical Bible*, Word (Speaker)

A topical Bible is an improvement over, but not a replacement for, a concordance. It lists for any word, person, or place the most prominent (if not all) passages. In some cases each biblical text will be written out in full, whereas at other times a certain subject will be exhaustively categorized for easy reference.

Bible encyclopaedia

* *The Zondervan Pictorial Encyclopaedia of the Bible*, Zondervan (Student and Speaker)

A Bible encyclopaedia is more complete than a Bible dictionary. It is more thorough in treatment and more comprehensive in subject matter handled.

Bible backgrounds

* James Freeman, *Manners and Customs of the Bible*, Logos (Student)
* Fred Wight, *Manners and Customs of Bible Lands*, Moody (Student)

* Alfred Edersheim, *The Life and Times of Jesus the Messiah*, Eerdmans (Speaker)

Bible history and culture is removed from us by thousands of years. Bible customs, manners, and mores are unknown to us except by books like these. They explain why people lived as they did.

To understand the life of a Palestinian shepherd makes Psalm 23 a living reality, and to understand the despicable nature of a tax collector magnifies Christ's grace shown towards Matthew. If you ever puzzled over the four soils in Matthew 13 or how a sick man could be lowered through a roof (Mark 2), then this kind of literary guide is essential for you.

Old Testament word helps

* W. E. Vine, *An Expository Dictionary of Old Testament Words*, Revell (Student)
* *Dictionary of New Testament Theology*, Zondervan Speaker)

The Bible is composed of words. These form sentences that are combined into paragraphs, whose whole leads to chapters and entire books. It is essential to know what a writer meant when he used a certain word.

Old Testament word helps explore the original meaning of Hebrew and Aramaic words and show how they were used in the everyday affairs of a person living at that time. Also these helpful guides explore how a certain word is used elsewhere in the Bible. Often this type of study clarifies a text and can provide rich illustrations.

New Testament word helps

*   W.E. Vine, *An Expository Dictionary of New Testament Words*, Moody (Student)
*   *Dictionary of New Testament Theology*, Zondervan (Speaker)
*   *Theological Dictionary of the New Testament* (abridged addition), Eerdmans (Speaker)

The Greek language by nature is more expressive than the Hebrew of the Old Testament. It is always a challenging and rewarding effort to dig into the heart of a New Testament word and discover its background. You will then have a clearer picture of what the Scripture writer meant.

Greek helps (Speaker only)

*   John Kohlenberger III, *The NIV Interlinear Greek-English New Testament*, Zondervan
*   Alfred Marshall, *The NASB Interlinear Greek-English New Testament*, Zondervan
*   Alfred Marshall, *The Interlinear Greek-English New Testament*, Zondervan (based on KJV)
*   J. Gresham Machen, *New Testament Greek for Beginners*, Macmillan.

You don't have to be a Greek scholar to begin enjoying the riches of the New Testament. By simply learning the twenty-four letters of the Greek alphabet, you can begin to use an interlinear Greek Testament and a basic Greek grammar. Thus you will have access to further study helps that are otherwise meaningless. The most important of these is the English-Greek concordance.

English-Greek concordance (Speaker only)

> *   *Englishman's Greek Concordance of the New Testament,*
>   various publishers

Often one Greek word is translated by several different English words. (The Greek word *hupomenō* is translated in the KJV as abide, endure, suffer, take patiently, and tarry behind.) Conversely, one English word can be translated by several different Greek words (four different Greek words are translated by the English word 'love').

Figures of speech helps (Speaker only)

> *   E.W. Bullinger, *Figures of Speech Used in the Bible,*
>   Baker

This is the only volume you will ever need to help with speech figures – it is exhaustive. It explains why the Bible says that God has wings (Ps. 91:4) and why God has eyes that run (2 Chron. 16:9). Did you ever wonder what Jesus meant when He invited the disciples to eat His body and drink His blood (John 6:53)? Or how a camel could go through the eye of a needle (Matt. 19:24)? Bullinger will give you good answers to what the Scripture writers meant by what they wrote.

Ethics volume (Speaker only)

> *   *Baker's Dictionary of Christian Ethics,* Baker

Christian doctrine is designed to lead into Christian living. It provides a biblical ethic by which we conduct the affairs of daily life. An ethics volume will provide a capsulized summary of the Bible teaching on abortion, war, marriage and divorce, homosexuality, sex, capital punishment, riches, and other subjects of contemporary interest.

Cross reference help (Speaker only)

*   *The Treasury of Scripture Knowledge*, Revell

Most Bibles give a few cross references to other texts that touch on the same subject. *The Treasury of Scripture Knowledge* is an exhaustive source of such references. It is essential for a complete picture of how your text fits into the rest of Scripture.

These resources will guide you safely through Scripture for a lifetime. In your journeys you will meet other study helps, books that will enhance Bible study even more. Don't be afraid to ask your pastor, a trusted friend, or the closest Christian bookstore for their recommendations.

A final note

My purpose in writing is not to do your Bible study for you but rather to encourage you to accurately study the Bible for yourself. I desire for you the joy of personal discovery in your travels through Scripture.

On the other hand, although good tools are essential, they are not enough. Method is equally important. Let us now turn to some practical helps for interpreting the Bible for yourself.

Questions for Discussion
1. Name the three levels of Bible interpretation research tools.

2. Which Bible version do you use? Why?

3. Describe the difference between a *translation* and a *paraphrase.*

4. What basic study tools are necessary to begin personal study and interpretation?

Four
Cutting It Straight for Yourself – Part 1

I RECENTLY READ an advertisement that claimed the Bible was the least read bestseller on the market. Why?

The thought of personal Bible study frightens most Christians. It seems to be so difficult without any formal training. Yet Psalm 119 persistently beckons every Christian to feed on the spiritual nourishment of Scripture.

Whether you are a pastor with several theological degrees or a new believer in Christ, a series of simple steps for fruitful Bible study can successfully lead you into the Word of God. You'll come away with the deep satisfaction of knowing that God has spoken to you through His Word and that you understand the message.

To illustrate how you can study the Bible for yourself, we'll use Psalm 13 as a sample text. This ancient poem could be entitled 'How to Wait for God.' It's an appropriate psalm for the twentieth-century speedster.

Armed with space-age computers, microwave cookery, and Instamatics, the 'now' generation wages a strong campaign against the old-fashioned virtue called patience. If you think it doesn't, just remember your last visit to a doctor's office or inching along in rush hour traffic.

God's plan marches to the cadence of an eternal clock – not the latest digit calibrated in microseconds. More often than not, God's time is slower than ours, as evidenced by how often we hurry up – only to wait. The Psalmist teaches us that 'timing' is everything in the divine execution of God's will for our lives.

Affirmation

Sir Walter Scott, on his deathbed, asked a friend to read to him. Puzzled, as he scanned the shelf of books that Scott had written, he asked, 'What book shall I read?' Sir Walter replied, 'Why do you ask that question? There is but one book; bring the Bible.'

Step one involves affirming that 'all Scripture is inspired by God and profitable for teaching, for reproof, for correction, for training in righteousness; that the man of God may be adequate, equipped for every good work' (2 Tim. 3:16-17). It is God's holy Scripture (Rom. 1:2).

The Bible does not compete with other books for the corner on truth. It is the truth (John 17:17). No book comes near as its equal. It is able to make one wiser than his enemies, provides more insight than all teachers, and gives more understanding than the aged.

> Thy commandments make me wiser than my enemies,
> For they are ever mine.
> I have more insight than all my teachers,
> For Thy testimonies are my meditation.
> I understand more than the aged,
> Because I have observed Thy precepts (Ps. 119:98-100).

Every time I open the Bible to study, it is with the fresh confession that it is 'God's Word.' Therefore, I accept it as inerrant (truthful) and infallible (trustworthy). It thus becomes my teacher and also my absolute authority for both belief and behaviour.

Preparation

When asked how to study the Scriptures most profitably, George Mueller remarked that he had two rules of thumb. First, prayerfully seek God's Spirit as primary teacher. Second, let the Holy Spirit teach at the appropriate time. That is to say, if an answer does not come immediately, keep seeking the Spirit's help.

John put it this way, 'And as for you, the anointing which you received from Him abides in you, and you have no need for anyone to teach you; but as His anointing teaches you about all things, and is true and is not a lie, and just as it has taught you, you abide in Him' (1 John 2:27). Paul concurs: 'For who among men knows the thoughts of a man except the spirit of the man, which is in him? Even so the thoughts of God no one knows except the Spirit of God' (1 Cor. 2:11).

Psalm 119 overflows with the writer's love of Scripture. We can learn much from his prayer. I have found the following sequence to be most meaningful in preparation to study.

1. 'Open my eyes that I may behold wonderful things from Thy law' (Ps. 119:18). It leads to knowledge.
2. 'Teach me Thy statutes' (Ps. 119:12). It leads to understanding.
3. 'Oh that my ways may be established to keep Thy statutes!' (Ps. 119:5). It leads to obedience.

Observation

Let's look at Psalm 13.

> [1]How long, O LORD? Wilt thou forget me forever?
> How long wilt Thou hide Thy face from me?

[2]How long shall I take counsel in my soul,
Having sorrow in my heart all the day?
How long will my enemy be exalted over me?

[3]Consider and answer me, O Lord, my God;
Enlighten my eyes, lest I sleep the sleep of death,
[4]Lest my enemy say, 'I have overcome him,'
Lest my adversaries rejoice when I am shaken.

[5]But I have trusted in Thy lovingkindness;
My heart shall rejoice in Thy salvation.
[6]I will sing to the Lord,
Because He has dealt bountifully with me.

Observe *singularly*; that is, at first do not look at any book
other than the Bible. Put God's Book in a place all of its
own. I try to read through a text scores of times before I
move ahead. Try this with Psalm 13.

Observe *carefully*. Spurgeon quotes from a writer of his
day: 'Most read their Bibles like cows that stand in thick
grass, and trample under their feet the finest flowers and
herbs.' Observe with the idea of discovering the detailed
beauty that God has put into His Word. Take your time
and concentrate.

Observe *thoroughly*. Start with the reminder that you will
never see it all at one study; but purpose to see as much as
you can.

One writer put it this way: 'It shall greatly help you to
understand Scripture, if you mark, not only what is spoken
or written,

But of whom?
And to whom?
With what words?

And what time?
Where?
To what intent?
With what circumstances?
Considering what goes before and after.'

Or in other words, observe both the content and the context.

Observe *systematically*. Martin Luther studied the Bible as one who gathered apples. 'First I shake the whole tree, that the ripest may fall. Then I climb the tree and shake each limb, and then each branch and then each twig, and then I look under each leaf.'

Observe *intimately*. Look at it with the realization you are reading a message from the heavenly Father to you His spiritual child. It's like a letter from home while you are far away.

As you observe you might begin to see the basic units of Psalm 13.

1. David's impatient complaint (13:1-2)
2. David's insistent cry (13:3-4)
3. David's indomitable confidence (13:5-6)

In 13:1-2, David asks five questions in a row. Four times he cries out, 'How long?' His repetitive protest immediately tells us David is fighting a battle with impatience.

The three questions in 13:1 seem to be asking:

1. Did God forget me (13:1a)?
2. Will it be forever (13:1b)?
3. Is something wrong with me (13:1c)?

13:2 takes on the form of a personal *protest* with these admissions:

1. I am frustrated (13:2a).
2. I feel forlorn (13:2b).
3. I see myself as a failure (13:2c).

There is a turn in the psalmist's voice at 13:3-4. He acknowledges his personal relationship with the one to whom he speaks: 'O LORD, my God.' His *protest* of 13:1-2 has led to this *prayer*.

13:4 alludes to possible circumstances that are the real life cause of the psalm. Later on we will see if it is recorded elsewhere in Scripture. It is a life and death matter.

Finally, in 13:5-6, the psalmist's *prayer* turns to *praise*. It raises the question, Why this dramatic change in response to life when the life circumstances that originally caused the *protest* have not changed?

Look carefully at the verbs in the last two verses. They follow this sequence – the past, the future, the future, the past. The psalmist begins to remember how God has dealt with him before and says, 'I must praise Him for that now and in days to come.' God's dealings with David in the past, when recalled, served to soothe and strengthen in the midst of current crisis.

Making the point

Look! That's the key to fruitful Bible study. We study at a well that will never run dry – so drink deeply of its life-giving provision.

Many years ago I read this fascinating and unforgettable story. It indelibly etched the importance of 'observation' in my mind. Your Bible study will be revolutionized if you apply the lesson taught by Professor J. Louis Agassiz.

The Student, the Fish, and Agassiz
By the Student

It was more than fifteen years ago that I entered the laboratory of Professor Agassiz, and told him I had enrolled my name in the scientific school as a student of natural history. He asked me a few questions about my object in coming, my antecedents generally, the mode in which I afterwards proposed to use the knowledge I might acquire, and finally, whether I wished to study any special branch. To the latter I replied that as I wished to be well grounded in all departments of zoology, I purposed to devote myself specially to insects.

'When do you wish to begin?' he asked.

'Now,' I replied.

This seemed to please him, and with an energetic 'Very well,' he reached from a shelf a huge jar of specimens in yellow alcohol.

'Take this fish,' said he, 'and look at it; we call it a Haemulon [pronounced Hem-yu lon]; by and by I will ask what you have.'

With that he left me, but in a moment returned with explicit instructions as to the care of the object entrusted to me.

'No man is fit to be a naturalist,' said he, 'who does not know how to take care of specimens.'

I was to keep the fish before me in a tin tray, and occasionally moisten the surface with alcohol from the jar, always taking care to replace the stopper tightly. Those were not the days of ground glass stoppers, and elegantly shaped exhibition jars; all the old students will recall the huge, neck-less glass bottles with their leaky, wax-besmeared corks half eaten by insects and begrimed with cellar dust. Entomology was a cleaner science than ichthyology, but the example of the professor, who had unhesitatingly plunged to the bottom of the jar to produce the fish, was infectious; and though this alcohol had 'a very ancient and fishlike smell,' I really dared not show any aversion within these sacred precincts, and treated the alcohol as though it were pure water. Still I was conscious of a passing feeling of disappointment, for gazing at a fish did not commend itself to an ardent entomologist. My friends at home, too, were annoyed, when they discovered that no amount of eau de cologne would drown the perfume which haunted me like a shadow.

In ten minutes I had seen all that could be seen in that fish, and started in search of the professor, who had, however, left the museum; and when I returned, after lingering over some of the odd animals stored in the upper apartment, my specimen was dry all over. I dashed the fluid over the fish as if to resuscitate it from a fainting-fit, and looked with anxiety for a return of the normal, sloppy appearance. This little excitement over, nothing was to be done but return to a steadfast gaze at my mute companion. Half an hour passed, an hour, another hour; the fish began to look loathsome. I turned it over and around; looked it in the face – ghastly; from behind, beneath, above, sideways, at a three-quarters' view – just as ghastly. I was in despair; at an early hour I concluded that lunch was necessary; so, with infinite relief, the fish was carefully placed in the jar, and for an hour I was free.

On my return, I learned that Professor Agassiz had been at the museum, but had gone and would not return for several hours. My fellow students were too busy to be disturbed by continued conversation. Slowly I drew forth that hideous fish, and with a feeling of desperation again looked at it. I might not use a magnifying glass; instruments of all kinds were interdicted. My two hands, my two eyes, and the fish; it seemed a most limited field. I pushed my finger down its throat to feel how sharp its teeth were. I began to count the scales in the different rows until I was convinced that that was nonsense. At last a happy thought struck me – I would draw the fish; and now with surprise I began to discover new features in the creature. Just then the professor returned.

'That is right,' he said, 'a pencil is one of the best of eyes. I am glad to notice, too, that you keep your specimen wet and your bottle corked.'

With these encouraging words he added, –

'Well, what is it like?'

He listened attentively to my brief rehearsal of the structure of parts whose names were still unknown to me: the fringed gill – arches and movable operculum; the pores of the head, fleshy lips, and lidless eyes; the lateral line, the spinous fin, and forked tail; the compressed and arched body. When I had finished, he waited as if expecting more, and then, with an air of disappointment, –

'You have not looked very carefully; why,' he continued, more earnestly, 'you haven't seen one of the most conspicuous features of the animal, which is as plainly before your eyes as the fish itself; look again, look again!' and he left me to my misery.

I was piqued; I was mortified. Still more of the wretched fish! But now I set myself to my task with a will, and discovered one new thing after another, until I saw how just the professor's criticism had been. The afternoon passed quickly, and when, towards its close, the professor inquired, –

'Do you see it yet?'

'No,' I replied, 'I am certain I do not, but I see how little I saw before.'

'That is next best,' said he earnestly, 'but I won't hear you now; put away your fish and go home; perhaps you will be ready with a better answer in the morning. I will examine you before you look at the fish.'

This was disconcerting; not only must I think of my fish all night, studying, without the object before me, what this unknown but most visible feature might be; but also, without reviewing my new discoveries, I must give an exact account of them the next day. I had a bad memory; so I walked home by Charles River in a distracted state, with my two perplexities.

The cordial greeting from the professor the next morning was reassuring; here was a man who seemed to be quite as anxious as I that I should see for myself what he saw.

'Do you perhaps mean,' I asked, 'that the fish has symmetrical sides with paired organs?'

His thoroughly pleased, 'Of course, of course!' repaid the wakeful hours of the previous night. After he had discoursed most happily and enthusiastically – as he always did – upon the importance of the point, I ventured to ask what I should do next.

'Oh, look at your fish!' he said, and left me again to my own devices. In a little more than an hour he returned and heard my new catalogue.

'That is good, that is good!' he repeated, 'but that is not all; go on.' And so, for three long days, he placed that fish before my eyes, forbidding me to look at anything else, or to use any artificial aid. 'Look, look, look,' was his repeated injunction.

This was the best entomological lesson I ever had – a lesson whose influence has extend to the details of every subsequent study; a legacy the professor has left to me, as he has left it to many others, of inestimable value, which we could not buy, with which we cannot part.

A year afterwards, some of us were amusing ourselves with chalking outlandish beasts upon the museum blackboard. We drew prancing star-fishes; frogs in mortal combat; hydra-headed worms; stately craw-fishes, standing on their tails, bearing aloft umbrellas; and grotesque fishes, with gaping mouths and staring eyes. The professor came in shortly after, and was as amused as any at our experiments. He looked at the fishes.

'Haemulons, every one of them,' he said. 'Mr... drew them.'

True; and to this day, if I attempt a fish, I can draw nothing but Haemulons.

The fourth day, a second fish of the same group was placed beside the first, and I was bidden to point out the resemblances and differences between the two; another and another followed, until the entire family lay before me, and a whole legion of jars covered the table and surrounding shelves; the odour had become a pleasant perfume; and even now, the sight of an old, six-inch, worm-eaten cork brings fragrant memories!

The whole group of Haemulons was thus brought in review; and, whether engaged upon the dissection of the internal organs, the preparation and examination of the bony framework, or the description of the various parts, Agassiz's training in the method of observing facts and their orderly arrangements was ever accompanied by the urgent exhortation not to be content with them.

'Facts are stupid things,' he would say, 'until brought into connection with some general law.'

At the end of eight months, it was almost with reluctance that I left these friends and turned to insects; but what I had gained by this outside experience has been of greater value than years of later investigation in my favourite groups.[3]

Questions for Discussion

1. What is involved in the principle of *affirmation*?

2. What do we mean when we say that the Bible is inerrant and infallible?

3. What are some ways we may prepare ourselves for studying the Bible?

4. Describe the four principles of *observation*.

5. Study Psalm 13. List your observations.

Five
Cutting it Straight for Yourself – Part 2

HERE IS a test. Observe the figure below for thirty seconds and write down how many squares you see.

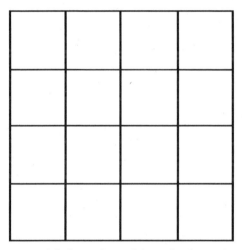

If you came up with less than thirty, look again. Stick with it until you can see them all. Now check your observations with the correct solution on page 199.

This challenging exercise in observation points out that there is more to see than first meets the eye. This is most true with the Bible. Every time we encounter Scripture, there will be new discoveries.

Studying Scripture is like mining and refining a precious metal. We are to continue working at the task until all is mined and then refined to its purest form. That is why the psalmist wrote, 'Therefore I love Thy commandments above gold, yes, above fine gold' (Ps. 119:127; cf. Ps. 19:10; 119:72). God has given each one of us a lifetime to observe the inexhaustible riches of His precious Word.

We've discussed the steps of affirmation, preparation, and observation so far. Now we add the remaining elements of 'cutting it straight' for yourself.

Investigation

After you have made your initial observation, it's time to see what other people have discovered. No one person holds a corner on discovering all that a passage contains. God has gifted many excellent teachers who have put their thoughts in print. They serve as a rich resource to the true Bible student.

You will want to use Bible atlases, Bible encyclopaedias, concordances, and commentaries. Also check out helps in theology, history, backgrounds, and the original language of Hebrew in the Old Testament and Greek in the New.

If you have questions, stop into your neighbourhood Christian bookstore to browse and ask for assistance. It could be your church has a library, or maybe you have access to a Bible college or seminary library.

I found the following commentaries very helpful in studying the Psalms: *Exposition of Psalms* by H.C. Leupold; *Psalms* by W.S. Plumer; *Psalms* by W. Graham Scroggie; and *Treasury of David* by Charles H. Spurgeon.

One Bible help I used outlined other people in the Bible who were despondent like David in Psalm 13. They included Moses (Num. 11), Joshua (Josh. 7), Elijah (1 Kings 19), Job (Job 3,10), Jeremiah (Jer. 20), and Habakkuk (Hab. 1).

Earlier we raised the question of what life circumstances caused David to pour out his heart to God. Biographical sketches of David or commentaries can be helpful here. As a teen David was anointed by Samuel to be king of Israel (1 Sam. 16). But it was not until aged thirty that he actually occupied the throne (2 Sam. 4-5). During this wait that exceeded a decade in time, Saul pursued David to kill him (1 Sam. 18-30). In all likelihood it was during this time that David screamed impatiently, 'How long, O LORD?'

Interpretation
What did God mean by what He said? That question is at the heart of interpretation. What is the true understanding of Psalm 13?

It all begins with a dependence upon God's Spirit for illumination. The psalmist confessed, 'For Thou Thyself has taught me' (Ps. 119:102).

Good interpretation employs the normal rules of literary interpretation. Interpret the Bible as you would any other kind of literature. It is the 'literal' method in that it takes the text at face value. Yet it recognises figures of speech and provides the only honest way to interpret the reality portrayed by symbol or imagery.

Daniel Webster once remarked: 'I believe that the Bible is understood and received in the plain obvious meaning of its passages, since I cannot persuade myself that a book that is intended for the instruction and conversion of the whole world should cover its meaning in any such mystery and doubt that none but critics and philosophers discover it.'

Interpretation takes *language* into consideration. It looks at words and their meaning, grammar, figures of speech, verb tenses, and so on. This bridges the gap between the

Hebrew of Psalm 13 and our English translation. Vine's *Expository Dictionary of Old Testament Words* is a helpful tool.

Interpretation looks at *culture.* How did they live when the text was originally written? What special customs, habits, or mores of their day would be helpful to understand? It helps to recreate the actual situation out of which a Scripture was written.

Geography is another prominent area in interpretation. Although it is not significant in Psalm 13, geography is very important if you are tracing the drama of David's escape from Saul or Paul's missionary journeys.

Interpretation always looks at *history.* All of the Bible occurs in the context of world history. This discipline is the time context in which to understand what God did with Israel in the Old Testament or the church in the New.

David Cooper puts it memorably: 'When the plain sense of Scripture makes common sense, seek no other senses; therefore take every word at its primary, ordinary, usual literal meaning unless the facts of the immediate context, studied in the light of related passages and axiomatic and fundamental truths, indicate clearly otherwise.'

Some of the interpretative issues raised in Psalm 13 are:

1. Can God really forget (13:1b)?
2. Does God have a face (13:1c)?
3. What does 'enlighten my eyes' mean (13:3b)?
4. What relationship does sleep have to death (13:3b)?
5. Who are David's enemies (13:2b, 4)?
6. What is God's salvation to David (13:5)?

One of the most important questions raised here is, Why was God silent? Why did God not immediately respond and rescue David? Interpretatively, the Bible teaches that there are several possible reasons for God's silence.

1. David was praying outside of God's will (1 John 5:14-15).
2. David did not have God's glory as his highest motive (1 Cor. 10:31).
3. Sin in David's life caused a prayer barrier (Isa. 1:15).
4. David had not yet been fully equipped by the circumstances, so God allowed them to continue (James 1:2-4).
5. It was not time yet to fully accomplish God's purpose (John 17:1).
6. God had a sovereignly concealed reason that David could not know (Deut. 29:29).

From the historical context of the psalm, it appears that either option 4, 5, or 6 is correct. Possibly it is some combination of the three.

The important thing to see is that God had purposes that went beyond what David could understand. Wrong motives, sin, seeking other than God's will were not the problem. It was getting in line with God's timetable – even if it meant waiting.

Correlation

In reality the Bible is actually one Book, not sixty-six. All thirty-nine books of the Old Testament and twenty-seven of the New are parts of 'The Book' we call God's Word.

So it is important when we study a text that we ask what else has God said about a certain theme or subject. How else has a certain word been used in Scripture? What else has happened in a location in biblical history? Is there anything else about the passage I can learn elsewhere in the Bible?

Correlation allows us to see the part (the text we study) in the light of the whole (the entire Bible). It provides the way to gain a proper biblical perspective – to major on majors and minor on minors. Once the whole is understood, the part will take on added meaning.

One of the best ways to do this is by using the cross references in your Bible to get a broader understanding. Chain reference Bibles are also helpful. The ultimate in tools to do this is *The Treasury of Scripture Knowledge.*

Psalm 13 raises the question, Is David the only person to question God with doubt? By correlation we discover David is in good company.

The prophet Habakkuk called out, 'How long, O LORD, will I call for help, and Thou wilt not hear?' (Hab. 1:2). John the Baptist despairingly queried, 'Are You the Coming One, or shall we look for someone else?' (Matt. 11:30). Even Christ anguished, 'My God, My God, why hast Thou forsaken Me?' (Matt. 27:46).

David was not the only saint who had to wait a considerable time for God's plan to fully unfold. He joined the elite ranks of Noah, who waited 120 years for the judgement of the flood (Gen. 6:3); Abraham, who waited 25 years for Isaac (Gen. 15-17); Moses, who waited 40 years to be rescued (Exod. 2:23-25; Acts 7:30); Joseph, who waited for over a decade to be vindicated (Gen. 37:2; 41:46); Job, who waited an indefinite period for restoration (James 5:11); and Daniel, who waited seventy years for God to intervene in Israel's history (Dan. 9:2).

If you want to expand on the idea of death's appearing to be like sleep, you can look at Jeremiah 51:39; Daniel 12:2; John 11:11-14; 1 Corinthians 11:30; and 1 Thessalonians 4:14.

Correlation helps flesh out the text. It provides depth and is a great source of illustration. Also it prevents us from drawing wrong conclusions from only part of what the Bible says. This expanded or theological emphasis constantly allows us to understand the part in light of its whole.

Personalization

The keys to application are the steps of *observation, investigation, interpretation,* and *correlation.* Until you have answered the question, What does the text mean by what it says? it is impossible to answer an even greater question, What does the text mean to me?

A great help in this realm of application is to memorize and meditate on the text. The Lord instructed Joshua: 'You shall meditate on it [the law] day and night, so that you may be careful to do according to all that is written in it' (Josh. 1:8). The psalmist was so eager for this that he wrote: 'My eyes anticipate the night watches, that I may meditate on Thy word' (Ps. 119:148). Paul admonished: 'Let the word of Christ richly dwell within you' (Col. 3:16).

When I was a new Christian someone shared a series of questions to ask of every Bible passage studied. They serve as catalysts in the process.

1. Are there *examples* to follow?
2. Are there *commands* to obey?
3. Are there *errors* to avoid?
4. Are there *sins* to forsake?
5. Are there *promises* to claim?
6. Are there *new thoughts* about God?
7. Are there *principles* to live by?

Psalm 13 is loaded with personal application. Let me prime your pump with a few ideas, and then you can add your own.

First, David did not abandon God in the midst of his impatience and questions. Rather, he sought God for a solution. Even though he started with protest, he came to the right person, and, because his focus was fixed on God, the conversation ended in praise.

Second, he did not try to redefine God as an explanation for how the Lord had responded to his circumstance. Instead, he affirmed God to be who God revealed Himself to be – a faithful Saviour.

Next, he did not publicly broadcast his innermost doubts about God's dealing with his circumstances. He chose to privately pray to God who really was the only One who could make a difference.

Fourth, David did not abandon reality. He didn't retreat or try to detour. He faced life squarely; he looked tough circumstances right in the eye.

Also, he did not get angry with God. Although there was initial protest, in short order David ended up worshipping God by praising His name.

Sixth, God was not indicted and put on trial by David.

The psalmist honestly testified that the problem was not with God but rather with his own lack of understanding of why God acted the way He did.

Finally, David did not plea bargain with God or try to coerce Him. Rather, he prayerfully asked for honest answers so he could live with understanding.

The step of *personalization* is summarized by Johann Albrecht Bengal: 'Apply thy whole self to the text; apply the whole text to thyself.' Our study of Scripture is never complete until what we know begins to direct how we live.

Appropriation

All of the steps so far have involved our intellect. These last two engage the will. To stop short here would be like driving ninety-five yards on the football field to your opponents' five-yard line, then deciding that touchdowns are unimportant and walking off the field, having wasted your previous labour with the goal not being reached. So near, yet so far.

Ask yourself, 'Am I obeying what I now know as a result of my personal Bible study?' This is the step that transfers the fruit of your labours from the head and heart to the hands and feet.

Jesus told the disciples, 'If you know these things, you are blessed if you do them' (John 13:17). 'But prove yourselves to be doers of the word, and not merely hearers who delude themselves' (James 1:22) was the mandate given by James. John promised, 'Blessed is he who reads and those who hear the words of this prophecy, and heed the things which are written in it; for the time is near' (Rev. 1:3).

Psalm 13 demands actions like, 'I will seek answers for my tough life from God!' 'I will praise God because of His past faithfulness even if today remains the same!' 'I will not abandon my faith in God regardless of what life throws at me!'

To do otherwise is to fail the test. God makes us accountable for what we know from His Word. James 4:17 makes our options clear: 'Therefore, to one who knows the right thing to do, and does not do it, to him it is sin.'

One of the greatest Bible teachers ever made this superlative statement: 'I have no greater joy than this, to hear of my children walking in the truth' (3 John 4). True joy comes with the exercise of our faith. Our challenge is to become the ultimate in 'living Bibles.'

Proclamation

Someone has claimed that true learning does not occur until the student is able to teach someone else what he has been taught. That is the genius of discipleship as outlined by Paul to Timothy: 'And the things which you have heard from me in the presence of many witnesses, these entrust to faithful men, who will be able to teach others also' (2 Tim. 2:2).

Ezra had three life goals. 'For Ezra had set his heart to study the law of the LORD, and to practise it, and to teach His statutes and ordinances in Israel' (Ezra 7:10). The culmination was to teach others what he had learned and mastered with his life.

I love the excitement of Andrew in John 1:40-41. He heard Christ teach and immediately sought out his brother, Peter, to tell him about Christ.

Listen to Peter's later exhortation: 'But sanctify Christ as Lord in your hearts, always being ready to make a defence to everyone who asks you to give an account for the hope that is in you, yet with gentleness and reverence' (1 Pet. 3:15).

This step demands that we form the habit of telling people what we have learned from God. So ask God to bring someone into your life on a daily basis with whom you can share your exciting discoveries in God's Word. Don't be silent about the most precious book ever written – someone's life might depend on it.

Potential candidates to hear your nugget of truth include:

* Dad or mom
* Husband or wife
* Son or daughter
* Friend
* Employer

* Fellow worker
* Neighbour
* Someone who waits on you

A final note

John Wesley read and reread the Bible through many times. In his old age he said, '*I am a homo unius libri.*' He was 'a man of one book.'

Let us walk in Wesley's footsteps!

Questions for Discussion

1. Describe the guidelines of investigation. What is its purpose?

2. What are the four components of interpretation? Why is each important?

3. How does correlation work? Why is it a helpful guideline?

4. Define personalization. What is its importance in the interpretation process?

5. What is unique about the guideline of appropriation?

6. Read 2 Timothy 2:2 and 1 Peter 3:15. Why is it important to carry our interpretation to the stage of proclamation? Consider your potential candidates for proclamation.

BIBLE STUDY WORKSHEET

Text:_____
Date:_____

Am I ready to study the text?
1. Affirmation: God's Word is inerrant and infallible. I can believe it all and depend upon it totally.

2. Preparation: I am studying to be approved by God, not ashamed before Him, because I cut the Word of Truth straight.

In dealing with my sin, Jesus Christ is my intercessor through whom I can restore pure fellowship with God.

The Holy Spirit is my divine illuminator, *i.e., teacher and guide.*

What does the text say?
3. Observation:

What does the text mean by what it says?
4. Investigation:

5. Interpretation:

What else does the Bible say about this text?
6. Correlation:

How does this text apply to me?
7. Personalization:

How has this text impacted my life?
8. Appropriation:

With whom can I share what I have learned?
9. Proclamation:

PART 2

AVOIDING CROOKED CUTS

Six

A Text Without a Context

ONE OF the theological bright spots of the 1980s was the conservative, evangelical movement to affirm the inerrancy of God's Word. Leading theologians and laymen at the grass-roots level rallied to affirm the absolute inerrancy of the Word of God in the face of a subtle attack by those who claim they believe the Bible yet say it contains factual errors. This tide has ebbed in the 1990s and is not nearly so strong in the twenty-first century.

The campaign to deny inerrancy is one of the most cunning and dangerous ploys ever devised by Satan because it defies the very basis of the Christian faith – the authority of the Word of God. Yet it is concealed under a veneer of scholarship, pseudo-belief, and evangelical language.

As dangerous as it is to deny inerrancy, however, it is worse to affirm inerrancy as a doctrinal position and then be careless in the practice of biblical interpretation. All too many who would gladly be martyred in defence of an inerrant Bible make their doctrine of no effect by erroneously interpreting Scripture. Thus they unwittingly preach and teach error from an inerrant Bible while believing themselves to be defenders of the historic, Christian faith concerning inerrancy.

It is interesting to note that the apostle Paul never argued polemically for the inerrancy of Scripture. Rather he assumed it and proclaimed it. He told Timothy that the Scripture is breathed out from God and able to teach, correct, and equip godly men for every good work (2 Tim. 3:16-17). In other words, we don't have to alter Scripture to bring it into harmony with truth; rather we need to allow Scripture to change the way we live so that the truth conforms us.

Paul admonished Timothy to devote his life to proclaiming the Word: 'Preach the word; be ready in season and out of season; reprove, rebuke, exhort, with great patience and instruction' (2 Tim. 4:2).

The apostle built on the foundation of his words in 2 Timothy 2:15, where he told Timothy that in order to present himself approved and unashamed to God, he must correctly interpret the Word of God: 'Be diligent to present yourself approved to God as a workman who does not need to be ashamed, handling accurately the word of truth.'

The word translated 'handling accurately' is the Greek word *orthotomeō*, which means 'cutting straight.' The word was used in Greek literature to describe the task of a guide, whose goal was to cut a straight path. It was also used to describe the work of a priest who sliced sacrificial animals according to divine instructions; of a farmer cutting a straight furrow; of a stonemason quarrying huge rocks so that they fit in the wall of a building; and of a tailor or tentmaker, who had to cut cloth.

In every case, the key idea is precision. Each of those tasks required exactness to the point of perfection.

And so it is with the sacred responsibility of interpreting the Word of God. We must cut it straight. We are handling God's Word, not our own. Our task is to herald, not to edit. We are stewards, not the ultimate authority.

We are to give it out just as God gave it, without altering its meaning or corrupting its purity in any way. What is demanded of us is faultless workmanship. We have to get it right.

That is not as easy as it sounds though. There are a number of hermeneutical pitfalls that threaten us as we study Scripture. Each of them represents a potential hazard in our pursuit of understanding what God's Word means.

Over the next few chapters, we'll expose some common hermeneutical obstacles to correct interpretation. They are commonly found in much of evangelical preaching today and need to be corrected.

Prooftexting

Every one of us has used the interpretive error of *prooftexting* to make a point. We string together an inappropriate or inadequate series of Bible verses to prove our theology.

Put another way – it is enticing, but wrong, to form one's theology apart from a complete inductive study of Scripture. It is wrong, having done this, to start looking for biblical texts that seem to support our conclusions, all without carefully interpreting the text to which we appeal.

Several years ago I was browsing through some commentaries in my favourite bookstore. A dear lady whom I had recently visited in the hospital entered and walked toward me. Greeting her, I remarked how well she looked. She responded, 'By His stripes I have been healed – praise God there is healing in Christ's atonement.'

Immediately I decided that the bookstore was no place for a theology discussion. I didn't want to dampen her new joy, nor did I want to rob her of her confidence that somehow God had been involved in her physical restoration. However,

her prooftexts – Isaiah 53:5 and 1 Peter 2:24 – just did not
describe what had happened to her. Let me explain.

Isaiah 53 refers primarily to the atonement and its
redemptive value, not its therapeutic effect in a physical
sense. Three lines of evidence support that reasoning:

1. The idea of atonement in Leviticus and Hebrews is
   applied primarily to salvation.
2. The context of Isaiah 53 focuses primarily on the
   atonement's provision for sin.
3. The theological context of Christ's death and salvation is centred primarily on sin.

Isaiah 53 primarily deals with the spiritual being of man.
Its major emphasis is on sin, not sickness. It focuses on
the moral cause of sickness, which is sin, and not on the
immediate removal of one of sin's results – sickness.

Matthew 8 is a limited and localized preview of a believer's experience in eternity, where sickness will be no
more because sin will be no more. Christ did not personally
bear sickness in Capernaum in a substitutionary way but,
instead, removed it. Matthew refers to Isaiah 53 for illustra-
tive purposes and by no means intends it to be understood
as meaning that the prophecy in Isaiah 53 was fulfilled two
years before Christ went to Calvary.

1 Peter 2:24 rehearses the primary redemptive implication
of Isaiah 53. Christ's atoning death provided the basis for
spiritual health and eternal life. Our iniquities were borne
by Christ to satisfy God's righteous demand against sin.
Physical health and healing are not primarily in view.

We ask, Is there healing in the atonement? My answer
is, 'Yes!' There is healing in the atonement, but it is never
promised to believers for the present. When sin is removed,

physical healing for believers will be in full but only in the future, when our bodies have been redeemed by the power of God (Rom. 8:23).

When we look at the language used, understand the context in which the above passages are found, see the com-plementing passages in Leviticus and Hebrews, and realize what was involved in the atonement, we can see that the atonement dealt with sin and the need to satisfy the righteous wrath of a just and holy God.

It will not be until sin is removed from our personal existence that you and I can have any hope of guaranteed physical well-being. When the full fruit of redemption is added to the present firstfruits, we will know the fullness of physical healing provided by the atonement.

In light of these facts, I wondered where my friend had found those prooftexts. Perhaps she had read or heard on television a faith healer's explanation of Isaiah 53. A friend or neighbour may have told her. But she did not get them from a careful study of Scripture, for these texts deal pre-eminently with our spiritual healing, not physical healing.

Another classic illustration focuses on those who are into 'naming it and claiming it'. One of their favourite texts is John 14:14, 'If you ask Me anything in My name, I will do it.' They insist that this verse and others (e.g. John 15:16; 16:23) give all Christians a license to name what they want and then to claim it by faith. It is reasoned that God is bound to provide, based on His prayer promises, because He cannot lie and will not go back on His promises.

They err in failing to recognize what the rest of Scripture says about prayer. They overlook the conditions that God places for answered prayer.

If we expect God to answer prayer, it must be in His will (1 John 5:14-15), not ours. We are to pray with an obedient heart (1 John 3:22) and to pray with right reasons, not selfish motives (James 4:1-3). This is in addition to Paul's blunt reminder that we do not know how to pray as we should (Rom. 8:26).

A careful look at all of Scripture, and not just specially selected texts, will protect us from presuming upon God with the misleading idea of 'naming it and claiming it.'

The gay community's prooftexting their sinful (not alternative) life-style from the Bible marks another major error. They misinterpret selected texts to make their point. Then they ignore clear Scriptures that unquestionably prohibit homosexuality, such as Leviticus 20:13; Romans 1:24-32; 1 Corinthians 6:9-11; and 1 Timothy 1:9-10.

David and Jonathan allegedly illustrate God's approval of male sexual relationships. Jonathan's great delight in David (1 Sam. 19:1) and their kissing each other (1 Sam. 20:41) are favoured texts.

Their appeal to Jesus as a homosexual is blasphemous. Because John leaned on Jesus' breast (John 13:23) and because John was the disciple whom Jesus loved (John 19:26; 21:7), they find support for homosexuality in the life-style of our Saviour.

Homosexuals fail to realize that a very valid non-romantic, nonsexual relationship can occur between males and between females. David and Jonathan, and our Lord and John, are holy examples of these most blessed friendships. Homosexuals have twisted Scripture by prooftexting to validate their warped affections.

The tragedy of making this interpretive error burned itself into my soul during a television debate I had with a female pastor. We both acknowledged the seven strategic biblical passages that deal with homosexuality (Gen. 19:1-11; Lev. 18:22; 20:13; Rom. 1:24-32; 1 Cor. 6:9-11; 1 Tim. 1:10 and Jude 7).

However, we came to diametrically opposed conclusions because the pastor defended her position with prooftexts instead of careful interpretation of each text in its context. She claimed, for example, that Leviticus 18:22 prohibited homosexuality as an element of worship, but outside of worship it was not prohibited. Her logic contained two major flaws. First, Leviticus 18 deals with life in general, not formal worship in particular. Second, her logic would lead her to conclude that outside formal worship child sacrifice (18:21), sodomy (18:23), and adultery (18:20) are legitimate activities too. But even she did not want to carry her reasoning to its logical conclusion.

To protect yourself from this common error, guard against starting with your own idea and then looking for biblical texts to support it. Always start with the Bible and draw out of it the mind of God. Also carefully interpret each individual text you use to defend or support a biblical truth. In so doing you will not be guilty of using an inappropriate or inadequate series of texts.

Isolationism

Closely associated with prooftexting, yet somewhat different, is *isolationism.* This occurs when we fail to interpret a single Scripture in light of its context. We isolate the Scripture from its immediate literary surroundings.

How many times have you heard someone claim an answer to prayer by quoting Matthew 18:19-20? 'Again I say to you, that if two of you agree on earth about anything that they may ask, it shall be done for them by My Father who is in heaven. For where two or three have gathered together in My name, there I am in their midst.'

If you look carefully at the verses, you will note that they are inseparably linked to Matthew 18:15-18. The two or three gathered have not assembled to pray but rather to enact church discipline.

Recently I participated on a radio talk show in Los Angeles. I was answering questions about healing based on my book *The Healing Promise*. A lady phoned and asked how I could possibly say that God is not healing through human healers today as He did through the prophets, Christ, and the apostles, in light of Jeremiah 30:17.

First, I had her look at the context of this verse before I answered. Then I explained this was God's promise to Israel, not to everyone who ever lived. Furthermore, the promise dealt with national restoration, not physical healing.

Her response remains forever lodged in my memory. 'If that is true, then how can a poor layperson like me ever hope to understand the Bible?' I shared with her the three most important rules for Bible study: (1) *context*, (2) *context*, and (3) *context*. This basic approach to Bible study will carry laypeople a long way towards understanding what God means by what He says in the Bible.

Further chapters will expand our thinking about context. However, let me urge you to study every passage in light of its historical context, cultural context, grammatical context, literary context, and theological context. This will prevent you from isolating your text from its context.

William Tyndale challenged the ignorant, careless clergy of his day with this thought: 'If God spares my life, before many years pass I will make it possible for a boy behind the plough to know more Scripture than you do.' Violent death marked Tyndale's end because of his up-front commitment to the Bible. He had shamed the clergy of his day because they poorly fed their flocks, and he fed the pure milk of God's Word to the hungry believers in his time.

Tyndale's legacy alone serves as a premiere motivation to get God's Word right, to understand and communicate correctly what God delivered inerrantly. Paul's mandate is even stronger – 'Cut it straight!'

Questions for Discussion

1. Read 2 Timothy 2:15 and 4:2. What truths can we learn from those verses?

2. Why is consideration of the context of a passage so important?

3. Define *prooftexting*. What is the danger of this error?

4. What are some examples of prooftexting?

5. Describe *isolationism*. How is this error often used in interpreting Matthew 18:19-20?

Seven

Adding to Scripture

RECENTLY A letter crossed my desk from a man in Pennsylvania who asked about Revelation 22:19. He wrote, 'I would really like to know what the Apostle meant; for it really bothers me to know what I am reading but not to understand it.'

He makes a great point. It's incredibly bothersome to have information, especially information from God, but not to know what it means or not to understand the demands on our lives.

This challenge has faced God's people through the ages. That is why Ezra and his band of trained Bible interpreters stood before the people and read from the law of God: 'And they read from the book, from the law of God, translating it to give the sense so that they understood the reading' (Neh. 8:8). They explained the sense of the text so that the people could understand their reading. Thus, God's Word could be carefully obeyed: 'And all the people went away to eat, to drink, to send portions and to celebrate a great festival, because they understood the words which had been made known to them' (Neh. 8:12).

Their challenge is ours today. That's why Paul exhorted Timothy to 'get it right' (2 Tim. 2:15); and that is why we continue our studies in rightly dividing the Word of God.

We have corrected two common mistakes – *prooftexting* and *isolationism*. Stringing together an inappropriate or inadequate series of Bible verses to prove a point rests at the heart of prooftexting. In contrast, isolationism involves the failure to correctly interpret a single Scripture text because the immediate context is ignored, that is, the text is isolated from its context.

Spiritualizing

Now let us turn to another frequent mistake – *spiritualizing*. This happens when we read a spiritual or historical truth *into* a text rather than extracting truth *from* it. Theologians call this 'eisegesis,' which literally means 'to lead into'.

You can see the problem. None of us wants to add to Scripture, but we inadvertently can if we are not very careful.

I will never forget a missionary coming to speak in chapel during my seminary days. He began by confessing that what he was about to do was wrong, that he had been taught better, and that the seminary faculty would cringe – but he would do it anyway.

He then proceeded to teach about the church from Esther. This Old Testament historical book became a spiritual drama for him that portrayed the struggle of the church against the forces of evil.

Even as a first year seminary student I knew that Esther had a lot to do with the Jewish struggle for survival in Persia but nothing to do with the New Testament church. Unless, of course, we take the liberty and insert the church, which was foreign to God's intention for Esther. This unique Old Testament historical book unmistakably teaches that the supremely sovereign hand of God is upon the Jewish race to preserve them.

Maybe you have heard a message from the Song of Solomon about the wonder of Christ's love for the church

His bride, when in fact this exquisite piece of Hebrew poetry highlights the sacred beauty of undefiled love between a husband and wife.

The names *Rose of Sharon* and *Lily of the valley* have been given to Christ, using Song of Solomon 2:1 as a scriptural basis. Children love the little chorus *His Banner over Me is Love*, taken from Song of Solomon 2:4. But there is nothing in the song that speaks of Jesus, nor is there any New Testament affirmation that the writer intended this book to speak of the Messiah.

When this material first appeared in an American magazine, there were several interesting responses. One person was distressed because I apparently did not see the Lord Jesus Christ in nearly every page of the Old Testament.

Anyone who reveres the Bible as I do knows that the Old Testament is filled with Christ:

> Now He said to them, 'These are My words which I spoke to you while I was still with you, that all things which are written about Me in the Law of Moses and the Prophets and the Psalms must be fulfilled' (Luke 24:44).

> You search the Scriptures, because you think that in them you have eternal life; and it is these that bear witness of Me (John 5:39).

But that does not mean that Christ appears on every page. To add Christ where He does not appear is to sincerely, but wrongly, add to Scripture.

Another person wrote suggesting that I had contradicted C. I. Scofield and Harry Ironside. Although these men have ably ministered to me and Christ's Body through their writings, we must always come back directly to the Word.

The better question is not, What did a well-known author teach?, but rather, What does God's Word teach?

All of us have read or listened to impassioned pleas to build a church building, using Exodus or Nehemiah as the biblical basis of exhortation. The truth of the matter is that in Exodus Moses was building the Tabernacle, and Nehemiah built a wall around Jerusalem. These texts were not given by God to teach about church buildings. They were given as a historical record to remind us of how God has accomplished His will through people.

Before we look to another category, let me expose the other side of the spiritualizing coin. Instead of reading a historical or theological fact into the text, spiritualizing is reading a wrong application into the text. This normally comes as a result of a wrong interpretation. Gideon's fleece is a classic (Judg. 6:36-40). Everyone who now 'puts out a fleece' to determine God's will has fallen into this spiritualizing trap. The fleece was for Gideon, not us. As a matter of fact, there is good reason to believe that Gideon's fleece demonstrated his lack of faith rather than a commendable 'walk of faith.'

The following story is true, but tragic. A recently married couple approached a Southern California pastor for help with their troubled marriage. As a part of the initial interview, the pastor asked, 'What convinced you that you should marry?'

The husband recounted how he had gone to his pastor, seeking to know the will of God for himself and his girl friend, now his wife. That pastor reminded the young man of how Joshua and the Jews had marched around Jericho several times and how the walls collapsed (Josh. 6:15).

Then the pastor suggested that the boyfriend literally walk around his girl seven times. If the walls of her heart collapsed then he could be sure God wanted him to take her for his wife.

So he obeyed, circled the girl several times, and popped the question, 'Have the walls of your heart tumbled?' She responded by saying she felt strange inside, so they both concluded her heart had fallen in love, and thus they made plans to wed.

Although this dramatic kind of experience does not happen every day (thankfully), it vividly illustrates just how important it is to accurately interpret Scripture. Whether the couple should have married or not is another question; but Joshua 6 was certainly not the text on which to base their decision.

Here are some tips on how to avoid the error of spiritualizing:

First, always read and interpret a passage in its literary and historical context. For example, read Joshua in its historical setting. You will discover that it is a record of how the Jewish race under Joshua's leadership recaptured the geographical territory that God had given to Abraham centuries before.

Knowing this, you will resist the temptation of seeing Joshua as the Ephesians of the Old Testament. Joshua does not teach that the church should be militantly triumphant, nor does Ephesians teach that the church should be victorious in a physical sense.

By consistently following this simple rule, you will never be guilty of making the Bible a literary vehicle to teach a truth beyond itself.

Next, consciously work hard never to read anything into the text. Consistently draw your thoughts from the passage. Take time right now and read the Song of Solomon. As you read, ask yourself what the text, at face value, is teaching. You will come away with the strong impression that it is a beautiful love song between a bridegroom and his bride. It's an expression of endearment between two individuals who are very much in love. You will discover that God's purpose for Song of Solomon was not to directly teach about the Lord Jesus Christ.

Third, work hard to distinguish between strict inter-pretation and possible applications. Think back to Gideon's fleece. Is there anything in the text that suggests it is God's recommended method of normally discerning His will? Is there anything in the passage that would encourage believers through the ages to use this method?

By strict interpretation, we discover it is the historical record of a one-time event in Gideon's life – that's all. Further, it could very well be an expression that illustrates Gideon's lack of faith rather than fullness of faith.

What do we learn by application from Gideon's experience? Consistent with New Testament teaching about God's will, it is obvious that when we have a clear word from God in the Bible, as Gideon had from the angel of the Lord (Judg. 6:11-18), we need to obey without hesitation. We also learn of God's patience with faltering faith. Although Gideon hesitantly pursued God's will, nonetheless he pursued it, and God worked through him. There are many more applications bound up in Gideon's example. They are based not on the exact experience but rather on such things as the never-changing character of God and the constant elements of life's experience.

As you follow these simple guidelines, you will never find the church in Esther or Christ in Song of Solomon. And you won't ever use a 'fleece' again when seeking God's will.

Having said this, some would accuse us of having used 'interpretative scissors' to cut out a part of the Old Testament. Nothing could be further from our intention, for the Scripture says, referring to the Old Testament:

> Now these things happened to them as an example, and they were written for our instruction, upon whom the ends of the ages have come (1 Cor. 10:11).

> For whatever was written in earlier times was written for our instruction, that through perseverance and the encouragement of the Scriptures we might have hope (Rom. 15:4).

> All Scripture is inspired by God and profitable for teaching, for reproof, for correction, for training in righteousness (2 Tim. 3:16).

However, that is not licence to make the Old Testament teach whatever we want it to teach. That's why careful study and special efforts to distinguish between strict interpretation and application are so important in the Old Testament.

Nationalizing

Although it is akin to spiritualizing, *nationalizing* is different enough to warrant our special attention. This type of misinterpretation happens when we see our own country as the recipient of national promises made by God in the Bible to Israel.

Nationalizing is commonly practised by Western evangelicals who in a moment of patriotic passion claim 2 Chronicles 7:14 for America. I love my country, served as a regular officer in the United States Navy for six years, and was decorated for service in Vietnam. But no matter how much I love America, I can't claim this text for the USA when God clearly gave it to another people.

Open your Bible to 2 Chronicles 7:14. You would do well to read 2 Chronicles 1–7 first. You will discover there that the context of 2 Chronicles encompasses the reign of Solomon over united Israel in the tenth century BC.

It is set in the context of the Temple being built by Solomon (2:1; 3:1; 5:1). After the sanctuary had been dedicated and celebrated (5:2–7:10), God then appeared to Solomon (7:12).

Earlier, when dedicating the Temple, Solomon had prayed much about God forgiving the sins of the nation (6:22-39). So God in 7:12-22 speaks to Solomon about sin, about blessing for repentance, about punishment if sin continued:

> Then the LORD appeared to Solomon at night and said to him, 'I have heard your prayer, and have chosen this place for Myself as a house of sacrifice. If I shut up the heavens so that there is no rain, or if I command the locust to devour the land, or if I send pestilence among My people, and My people who are called by My name humble themselves and pray, and seek My face and turn from their wicked ways, then I will hear from heaven, will forgive their sin, and will heal their land. Now My eyes shall be open and My ears attentive to the prayer offered in this place. For now I have chosen and consecrated this house that My name may be there forever, and My eyes and My heart will be there perpetually. And as for you, if you walk before Me as your father David walked even to do according to all that I have commanded you and will keep My statutes and My ordinances, then I will establish your royal throne as I covenanted with your father David, saying, "You shall not lack a man to be ruler in Israel."

'But if you turn away and forsake My statutes and My commandments which I have set before you and shall go and serve other gods and worship them, then I will uproot you from My land which I have given you, and this house which I have consecrated for My name I will cast out of My sight, and I will make it a proverb and a byword among all peoples. As for this house, which was exalted, every one who passes by it will be astonished and say, "Why has the LORD done thus to this land and to this house?" And they will say, "Because they forsook the LORD, the God of their fathers, who brought them from the land of Egypt, and they adopted the other gods and worshipped them and served them, therefore He has brought all this adversity on them." ' (2 Chron. 7:12-22)

Don't miss this! God's promise to Solomon and Israel has nothing to do with America or any other country where Christians live today. No matter how spiritual or unspiritual America becomes, the outcome of our national history will not rest on the conditions of 2 Chronicles 7:14 but rather on the sovereignty of God: 'And it is He who changes the times and the epochs; He removes kings and establishes kings; He gives wisdom to wise men, and knowledge to men of understanding' (Dan. 2:21).

I once received this response to my comments on 2 Chronicles 7:14: 'As for 2 Chronicles 7:14, if those marvellous words don't apply to America (or Russia or Great Britain) as clearly as they did to Israel in Solomon's day, then I'm going to lay down my Old Testament because it doesn't mean anything in the 20th century.'

Let's think about that for a moment. Do all of the promises of the Old Testament apply in the twentieth century as they did when they were first given? Does that mean that God could not make a promise individualized for a certain person or country at a particular time without its applying directly throughout the remainder of history?

The real issues to deal with when interpreting these promises are:

1. The character of God
2. The content and context of His promises

Some of God's promises are based on His never-changing character. One such promise, based on God's holiness and desire that all be holy (Lev. 19:2; 1 Pet. 1:15-16), is Psalm 15:

> ¹O LORD, who may abide in Thy tent?
> Who may dwell on Thy holy hill?
> ²He who walks with integrity, and works righteousness,
> And speaks truth in his heart.
> ³He does not slander with his tongue,
> Nor does evil to his neighbor,
> Nor takes up a reproach against his friend;
> ⁴In whose eyes a reprobate is despised,
> But who honors those who fear the LORD;
> He swears to his own hurt, and does not change;
> ⁵He does not put out his money at interest,
> Nor does he take a bribe against the innocent.
> He who does these things will never be shaken.

Other of God's promises are based on the content of the promise. For example, God's promise to never flood the earth again is just as true today as it was when given to Noah: 'And I establish My covenant with you; and all flesh shall never again be cut off by the water of the flood, neither shall there again be a flood to destroy the earth' (Gen. 9:11). Yet there are promises, as in 2 Chronicles 7:14, that are not based on God's eternal character alone but also on His specific will. There is nothing in this promise to Solomon for Israel that contains all-inclusive language as does the promise to Noah in Genesis 9:11. Nor does God's character guarantee national restoration because of revival.

The misapplication of promises is the underlying error of thought that leads the World-wide Church of God to teach that America and England are now the possessors of God's promises originally made to Israel.

Also this same mistake undergirds the Mormon belief that when Christ returns, it will not be to the Mount of Olives on the eastern slopes of Jerusalem (Zech. 14:4; Acts 1:11-12). Rather they teach His coming will be to Independence, Missouri. Much of Mormon literature points to Independence as the final Zion mentioned in the Bible. This is a classic example of a religious group founded in America that sees the culmination of history focusing on America rather than on Israel as taught in the Bible. This is because they have nationalized away the truth of Scripture by reading an idea into Scripture rather than asking, What does the text teach?

My point in referring to this error by some is that we should be doubly careful not to make the same mistakes they make. The groups mentioned have misinterpreted the Bible. We of all people need to guard against this kind of error and its ultimate consequences.

One final illustration will make the point. This question is asked frequently, Is the United States or Britain specifically referred to in biblical prophecy? I'm sure we would like to think our nation so prominent, and the time of Christ's return so imminent, that it surely must be mentioned.

One rather well-known teacher of prophecy believes he has located America in Isaiah 18. He sees the 'wings' in 18:1 referring to the wings of a bald eagle, which is our country's national emblem. The sending of ambassadors, he believes, refers to the extensive diplomatic corps dispersed world-wide by the State Department in Washington, D.C. So goes the reasoning.

However, a careful search of Isaiah 18 points not to modern America but rather to ancient Cush. If the context had been consulted, it would be obvious that Isaiah 13 through 23 refers to God's predicted judgements on such ancient people as the Babylonians, Moabites, Egyptians, and Cushites. Be careful to consult the context – its advice will save you from serious error.

Therefore, as you study the Old Testament, be particularly careful. Many national promises are given to Israel by God. Understand they are for Israel and no one else. Some of them God will fulfil in the future for Israel. None of them will God fulfil for other countries.

A final note

Several years ago, someone who realized how dearly I love the Scriptures presented to me a plaque bearing the following statements:

The Bible

This book contains: the mind of God, the state of man, the way of salvation, the doom of sinners, and the happiness of believers.

Its doctrine is holy, its precepts are binding, its histories are true, and its decisions are immutable. Read it to be wise, believe it to be saved, and practise it to be holy. It contains light to direct you, food to support you, and comfort to cheer you. It is the traveller's map, the pilgrim's staff, the pilot's compass, the soldier's sword, and the Christian's character. Here heaven is open, and the gates of hell are disclosed.

Christ is the grand subject, our good its design, and the glory of God its end. It should fill the memory, rule the heart, and guide the feet.

Read it slowly, frequently, and prayerfully. It is a mine of wealth, health to the soul, and a river of pleasure. It is given to you here in this life, will be opened at the judgement, and is established forever.

It involves the highest responsibility, will reward the greatest labour, and condemn all who trifle with its contents. It reminds me daily 'to cut it straight.'

Questions for Discussion
1. Define *spiritualizing*. What is the danger of this error?

2. What are ways we can avoid spiritualizing?

3. Why is it so easy to *nationalize* a passage?

4. Read 2 Chronicles 7:14. Using the guidelines learned earlier, how should that verse be interpreted?

5. What different kinds of promises do we find in the Bible? What is the proper approach in dealing with biblical promises?

Eight

Editing God's Mind

*D*o *not fold, bend, staple, spindle, or mutilate* is a phrase we usually associated with computer cards in an earlier age of technology.

But it is also an effective paraphrase of Paul's command to Timothy to interpret the Bible carefully: 'Be diligent to present yourself approved to God as a workman who does not need to be ashamed, handling accurately the word of truth' (2 Tim. 2:15).

The psalmist shared the same reverence for Scripture: 'Thy word is very pure, therefore Thy servant loves it' (Ps. 119:140). 'The sum of Thy word is truth, and every one of Thy righteous ordinances is everlasting' (Ps. 119:160).

That's why Paul exhorts Timothy, and us by application, to interpret the Bible carefully so that we can accurately understand what God meant by what He said and thus communicate it correctly. Scripture demands reverence, diligence, and commitment.

Our studies on interpreting the Bible stress the importance of correctly understanding Scripture. For what value is an errorless Bible if we preach an errant message from it?

Evangelicals frequently proclaim their love of Scripture and defend its inerrancy. But we must also demonstrate that love by interpreting Scripture's message with the care and concern it deserves.

There are limitless ways to mar the Bible's message. Liberals have denied certain prophetic portions by claiming they were written after the fact, not before. They also disclaim certain distasteful doctrines like man's sinfulness and need of a personal Savior. Liberals have tried to edit God's message.

Cults add to biblical revelation with supposed messages from God. Sometimes they are oral; other times they are written, as in the case of *The Book of Mormon*.

But before we become too smug, let me address another way the Bible is questioned. It strikes closer to home. I call it the 'hypocritical attack'. It is the error made by those of us who believe, preach, and fight for inerrancy but who carelessly handle Scripture and thus incorrectly interpret the Bible. We are all susceptible to this too frequent mistake if we do not consciously guard against it.

Put another way – when we interpret the Bible there is to be no deviation, no falsification, no change, no perversion, no mutilation, no altering, no destroying, no adding to, and no taking away from God's wonderful Word (Deut. 4:2; 12:32; Prov. 30:6; Rev. 22:18).

So far we have looked at the interpretive errors of prooftexting and isolationism. Next we discussed spiritualizing, which occurs when we read a spiritual or historical truth into a text or misapply what is taken from the text. Nationalizing, or seeing one's own country as the recipient of national promises made by God in the Bible to Israel, was also discussed.

Embellishing

Now we turn to a fifth common pitfall – *embellishing*. This occurs when we read current thinking into the Bible. We all strain at times to make the Bible seem more contemporary by garnishing Scripture's truth with the latest in modern thought.

Take the subject of creation for instance. Ever since the days of Darwin there has been great pressure brought by the scientific community to explain origins according to the latest scientific theory.

Although science has certainly made great contributions to understanding our world, we must insist upon beginning with biblical data in order to know the hows of our beginning. Whatever we conclude must result from our initial interpretation of Scripture rather than understanding Scripture through the aid of science. A grammatical interpretation of Genesis is primary to an accurate interpretation of the time in creation.

However we understand Genesis 1–2, we must begin with these salient biblical facts:

1. The Hebrew word for *day*, when accompanied by a numerical adjective (e.g. fourth day), is never used figuratively. It is always understood normally.
2. The Hebrew plural for *day* is never used figuratively in the Old Testament (Exod. 20:9) outside of a creation context. We are therefore led to believe that it is used in the same way when referring to origins.
3. The terms *evening* and *morning* are never used figuratively in the Old Testament. They always describe a twenty-four-hour period.
4. God actually defines day in Genesis 1:5 by designating it as a period of light and a period of darkness. After creating light (Gen. 1:3) and causing a spatial separation between the darkness and the light (with

respect to the earth; Gen. 1:4), God established the
light/dark cycle as a principal measurement of time;
that is, one day (Gen. 1:5). This light/dark cycle
is best understood as one full earth rotation, or a
twenty-four-hour day.

The grammatical interpretation of Genesis is primary
to an accurate interpretation of Scripture. These biblical
facts are significant exegetical indicators of the time aspect
manifested in creation. They point to creation in six con-
secutive twenty-four-hour days.

It is most important that we insist on not reading science
into the Bible. We must guard against letting a natural
science void a sure, exegetical interpretation of Scripture
just because there is an apparent conflict.

Psychology is another good example. With the positive
emphasis upon Christians comforting, exhorting and even
confronting one another, in counselling comes the danger
that we will attempt to understand the deepest needs of
humanity by interpreting the Bible aided by psychology
rather than by good interpretation of Scripture.

Robert Schuller's book *Self-Esteem: The New Reformation*
is a prominent example, so much so that, in its foreword,
University of Chicago scholar Martin Marty asks, 'Is not
this a philosophy which makes room for God more than a
theology that incorporates psychology?' This is exactly
what results when the Bible is interpreted by psychology
rather than psychology by Scripture.

The popular 'self-love' concept arises out of this same
mistake. Walter Trobisch cites Matthew 22:39 in his book
Love Yourself (p. 11) and notes: 'We find that the Bible
confirms what modern psychology has recently discovered:

without self-love there can be no love for others. Jesus equates these two loves, and binds them together, making them inseparable.'

However, Jay Adams has astutely observed that in Matthew 22 Jesus speaks of two commands: loving God and loving our neighbour. There is no third command to love ourselves. As a matter of biblical record, there is no command in Scripture to love ourselves. At times, it appears that the basis for self love comes more from Abraham Maslow's hierarchy of needs than from the Bible.

Let's look for a moment at what Jesus actually said.

> But when the Pharisees heard that He had put the Sadducees to silence, they gathered themselves together. And one of them, a lawyer, asked Him a question, testing Him, 'Teacher, which is the great commandment in the Law?' And He said to him, 'You shall love the Lord your God with all your heart, and with all your soul, and with all your mind. This is the great and foremost commandment. And a second is like it, You shall love your neighbor as yourself. On these two commandments depend the whole Law and the Prophets' (Matt. 22:34-40).

Christ's major emphasis is not on 'other love' or 'self love' but on 'God love.' He reinforces what Moses taught in Deuteronomy 6:5: 'And you shall love the LORD your God with all your heart and with all your soul and with all your might.' The starting point involves a right dynamic relationship with God. May I add that if you are truly right with God you will have a right relationship with self. That's why Christ did not need to command that.

The real problem will be with others. That's why the second commandment in Matthew 22:39 is quoting

Leviticus 19:18. James calls it the 'royal law' (James 2:8). It
is really what Christ had taught earlier in Matthew 7:12.
The major truth here focuses on others, not self.

So Jesus is not here teaching 'self love'. He is teaching
'God love,' which should be expressed in love to others.
To put it any other way is to be self-centered rather than
God-centered.

Prophecy is a third area of biblical study that can be
distorted by embellishing. Covenantalists err by reading
history into Scripture, whereas dispensationalists go wrong
by introducing current events.

Let me illustrate by looking at Albert Barnes' explanation
of Revelation 11:13. The 'earthquake' is understood as
the shock produced through Europe by the boldness of
Martin Luther and his fellow labourers in the Reformation.
The 'tenth of the city' that fell is identified as the sudden
falling away by a considerable portion of the colossal papal
power. Finally, the 7,000 people killed, according to Barnes,
refers to the number of people killed in papal Europe in the
wars that were consequent on the Reformation. A careful
reading of Revelation 11, however, gives no warrant for
such a specific historical analysis unless, of course, history
embellishes the biblical text.

The Olivet Discourse (Matt. 24–25) is a supremely important biblical text relating to prophecy. William Hendrickson,
normally a very excellent commentator, slips at this point
by embellishing the text with history. 'Wars and rumors
of wars' (Matt. 24:6) refers to all wars since the fall of
Jerusalem, he claims. He does the same kind of historical
analysis with 'famines and earthquakes' in Matthew 24:7.

Even more noticeable is Hendrickson's handling of
24:14. The preaching of the gospel in the whole world is

said to be the history of Christianity's spread from the first century until today. Let me suggest it would be better to leave our understanding of a text vaguely broad rather than be factually specific by weaving history into the Bible when there is no scriptural warrant for such details of the past.

Dispensationalists make a variation of this error by reading current events into the text. One writer has aptly labelled this technique 'newspaper exegesis'.

Recently, this comment on the Olivet Discourse crossed my desk: 'As you know, there are a lot of Christians, including myself, who believe that the generation which saw Israel become a nation in 1948 "will not pass away" until the Lord comes again in the Rapture and again at the end of the tribulation period. This belief is based on Matthew 24, particularly verses 32–34.'

What the writer did not realize is that Jesus was not using the fig tree to represent Israel. If you look at the parallel passage in Luke 21:29, Jesus illustrates the point with 'the fig tree and all the trees'. Thus, our Lord's point has nothing to do with the establishment of the state of Israel in 1948, but rather He draws an analogy from nature. He makes the point that just as fig trees, or any other non-evergreen tree, bud in late spring and thus announce the coming of summer, so the appearance of signs precedes and portends the time when Christ's second coming is imminent.

When Israel defeated their Arab enemies in the Six-Day War of 1967, many dispensationalists suggested that Luke 21:24 had been fulfilled. Israel's repossession of Jerusalem for the first time in 1,900 years is surely what this text pointed to. However, if we compare Luke 21:24 carefully with Revelation 11:2, we discover they are parallel passages. That means, in my view, that this prophecy concerning 'the time of the Gentiles' will not be fulfilled until the end of the 'forty-two months', or during the Tribulation period.

With these illustrations in mind, let me suggest some practical steps that every conscientious interpreter of the Bible can follow to reduce the error of embellishing:

1. Every time you come to Scripture warn yourself about the danger of embellishing.
2. Pray that our Lord would keep you from error and guide you into the truth (Ps. 119:18).
3. Approach the text as though you are studying it for the first time. Take a fresh look free from previous bias.
4. Start with the biblical text, not with an outside discipline.
5. Let the text speak for itself.
6. Don't be afraid to let the Bible, not other fields of study, have the last word.

Methodologizing

Our next error is usually made by scholars, not the Christian layman. It is included here to warn the unwary student of Scripture not to use the materials produced by persons who employ this highly suspect method of interpretation.

Methodologizing occurs when the Scriptures are interpreted by means of an unproved theory about the Bible's literary origin. Scholars have hypothesized about how or why a part of the Bible came into existence and then used their theory to interpret the text. This is particularly true with studies in the Gospels.

Redaction critics, for the most part, do not embrace traditional viewpoints of authorship. They look upon the originators of the synoptics as later theological editors to whose works the names of Matthew, Mark, and Luke were attached for the sake of prestige. These anonymous compilers are, then, the ones whose theological views are in question in this type of research. Such views are assumed to be quite distinct from any specific, systematic teaching delivered by Jesus. [+]

Yet, there is not one shred of substantial evidence (historical or biblical) that this is how the Gospels came into being. And until the theory can be conclusively proved, it should be rejected as a legitimate means to interpret Scripture.

Robert Gundry in *Matthew: A Commentary on His Literary and Theological Art* develops a hybrid form of redaction criticism. He does support Matthew's authorship (pp. 609-622) and a traditional writing date (pp. 599–629), unlike many others. Yet he assumes that Matthew employed a particular editing methodology that caused him to 'depart from the actuality of events' (p. 623) and to 'materially alter and embellish historical traditions' (p. 639).

The best way to prevent this error is to ignore it. Redaction criticism, or *redaktionsgeschichte*, is an unproved theory and should not be used to interpret Scripture. You would be wise to steer clear of reading men who use this method to interpret the Bible.

John Wycliffe was a scholarly man deeply concerned over correct biblical interpretation. He is known affectionately as the 'morning star of the Reformation'. This fourteenth century Oxford professor led the way for Scripture to be released from sole possession of the Roman Catholic hierarchy to the common men of his day.

Because of Wycliffe's commitment to correctly interpreting the Bible, even if it overturned centuries of tradition, he became an enemy of the church. Although he was not martyred as others, forty-four years after his natural death the church exhumed his body, burned his bones, and scattered the ashes in a nearby river.

Before he died Wycliffe wrote:

> Christ and His apostles taught the people in the language best known to them. It is certain that the truth of the Christian faith becomes more evident the more faith itself is known. Therefore, the doctrine should not only be in Latin but in the vulgar tongue and, as the faith of the church is contained in the Scriptures, the more these are known in a true sense the better. The laity ought to understand the faith and, as doctrines of our faith are in the Scriptures, believers should have the Scriptures in a language which they fully understand.

The Bible we have today has been handed down to us from the apostles through multiplied generations of men like John Wycliffe. They labored, fought for, and even died over the issue of God's people having God's Word and correctly understanding what God taught.

Now it's our turn to pass this marvellous legacy on to another generation. So let's 'cut it straight!'

Questions for Discussion

1. What does 'editing God's mind' mean?

2. In what ways does *embellishing* mistreat Scripture?

3. Read Matthew 22:34–40. How is the popular self-love concept a result of embellishment?

4. What are some ways we can reduce the error of embellishing?

5. Define *methodologizing*. What issue is this error often associated with?

6. Why is methodologizing dangerous?

Nine

Modernizing the Bible

IN *THE GREAT EVANGELICAL DISASTER* the late Francis Schaeffer places the 'cookies' on the lower shelf of the inerrancy issue. 'I would ask again, does inerrancy really make a difference – in the way we live our lives across the whole spectrum of human existence?'

'No!' responds George Gallup, the famous American pollster. 'We find there is very little difference in ethical behaviour between church goers and those who are not active religiously ... The levels of lying, cheating and stealing are remarkably similar in both groups.'

Shocking. But true. So in this chapter we are going to discuss several more common errors in interpretation; they explain part of the 'why' for Gallup's alarming observation.

Most of us consider Jehoiakim's destroying the Bible unacceptably radical. 'And it came about, when Jehudi had read three of four columns, the king cut it with a scribe's knife and threw it into the fire that was in the brazier, until all the scroll was consumed in the fire that was in the brazier' (Jer. 36:23).

But there is another danger that deceivingly seems acceptable to many. Either way violates God's intentions for His inerrant Word.

A group of men told Jeremiah: 'Pray ... that the LORD your God may tell us the way in which we should walk and

the thing that we should do' (Jer. 42:1-3). Jeremiah returned
with God's direction, 'Do not go into Egypt.'

But that was not the answer they wanted. So they
rebelled and rationalized their disobedient desires by calling
Jeremiah a liar and going to Egypt anyway (Jer. 43:2-7).
They accommodated God's will to their own.

Accommodation

Accommodation is viewing Scripture through the lens of
human reason. This doesn't have to take the form of denying
the supernatural. It is also manifested in the subtle practice
of diluting the full impact of the Scripture to accommodate
or excuse sinful behaviour. Perhaps we've all been guilty of
that at one time or another.

Several years ago my wife had the opportunity to counsel
a young girl, an unmarried student at a Christian college,
who had become pregnant. She came to our home and
poured her heart out to my wife, who asked me to talk with
her. I asked her if she realized that the relationship she had
was sinful.

I was amazed by her response. She said, 'There's nowhere
in the Bible that it says that it's sinful to have a physical
relationship outside marriage between two people who love
one another.'

Admittedly not one verse uses those exact words, but
she had nonetheless rationalized Scripture. The intent of
passages like 1 Thessalonians 4:3 – 'This is the will of God,
your sanctification; that is, that you abstain from sexual
immorality' – is very clear (also 1 Corinthians 7:2). Physical
love outside of marriage is sin.

This news caption appeared in a religious periodical: 'Sex
outside marriage is acceptable for an elderly man and woman

whose financial situation makes marriage impossible.' This was the studied opinion of clergy and laity in a well-known American denomination.

A Christian college professor divorced his wife for another woman, accelerating the marital fracture with adultery. Several years have passed, and he now pastors a growing church. This man has concluded that because there is fruit in his church, God has affirmed his unbiblical divorce and remarriage as right.

But fruit is not necessarily a sign of God's blessing. At times it becomes a demonstration of God's mercy. Take Samson for instance. God used him mightily in spite of his sins (Judges 14–16). That is God's sovereign choice but not always His sign of pleasure.

In each of these cases, the obvious teaching of Scripture has been accommodated to the desired life-style of the rationalizing Christian. It is more an issue of the will than just possession of the right knowledge. It is a case where clear biblical content ought to dictate the shape of our Christian character.

Biblical accommodation is no different from Joseph Fletcher's 'situational ethics'. It reasons that absolutes must bow when personal situations warrant. In effect, God's perfect Word is set aside in favour of man's imperfect will.

For many, however, the issues of morality are inviolable. But what about attitudes and emotions?

Take James 1:19-20 for instance: 'This you know, my beloved brethren. But let everyone be quick to hear, slow to speak and slow to anger; for the anger of man does not achieve the righteousness of God'; or, 'Be angry, and yet do not sin; do not let the sun go down on your anger, and do not give the devil an opportunity' (Eph. 4:26-27).

We are all tempted to accommodate our Vesuvius-type outbursts as 'righteous anger'. Prolonged anger is excused by 'I can't help it' or 'They deserve it' or 'It's good to vent'.

Don't miss this. A righteous end never justifies an unrighteous means. A fruitful church ministry does not justify an unbiblical divorce. Love does not justify a sexual encounter outside of marriage. A wrong suffered does not justify sinful anger or an 'I'll get even' attitude.

Another growing area of accommodation is legal retaliation for a wrong suffered. I recently met with a businessman and a professional athlete who had entered into a business relationship. Through a series of financial setbacks, a great deal of money was lost.

Each man felt betrayed. One of the participants seriously considered legal action. Based on the prohibition in 1 Corinthians 6:1-7 against lawsuits between Christians and the admonition in Ephesians 4:32 to forgive as Christ forgave, one man forgave the other of a monetary sum in six figures. They also forgave each other for all the reactionary attitudes and words.

They were tempted by the pressure of our society to capitulate – to accommodate Scripture. But daring to trust God and obey, they won by losing. They willed to obey what they knew to be right in God's sight.

The best way to protect against the real danger of accommodation is to know your Bible by spending regular time studying it (Job 23:12). Then commit yourself to be a doer of the Word (James 1:22-25). To do otherwise is to sin (James 4:17).

Culturalizing
Societal demands produce great pressure to 'restudy' and 'rethink' time-honoured doctrines because they do not march

to the beat of contemporary drummers. *Culturalizing* limits a text to a specific time in history or culture, when in reality the text demands a wider application in time.

Some examples of biblical issues susceptible to this kind of error include:

* Anointing services in James 5:14–20
* Husband leadership in Ephesians 5:22–24
* Male elders in 1 Timothy 2:11–12

I once participated in a televised panel discussion on 'The Role of Women in the Church'. Early in the program it became obvious that the real issue was biblical authority. I wanted to insist that the Bible be our only source of instruction, not the Bible plus some other book.

In response, a mainline denomination pastor agreed to limit our discussion to Scripture and then immediately dismissed 1 Timothy 2:11–12 as being the product of a male-dominated society. He reasoned that because we live in a different era, this text has no bearing or authority on the issue of church leadership.

That is a convenient way to insist on 'Scripture only' and then take what you want and reject what is objectional. What this pastor failed to deal with in the text were certain facts that left no doubt that 1 Timothy 2 does not contain time limitations. This is a classic case of culturalizing, which in effect made him the editor of God's mind.

By following some basic steps, you can successfully avoid the hazard of culturizing. First, ask, 'Are there any time indicators in the text?' For example, in 1 Timothy 2:11–15

Paul teaches about male leadership in the church. Yet, many insist that the intent of the passage is limited to the patriarchal society of the first century. But Paul appeals to the beginning of time (creation and Fall) in supporting his conclusion. Thus the basis of his instruction is as valid today as it was in the first century.

In the case of James 5 there is no limiting time indicator. Therefore, to assume that this passage is not for today is to wrongly read a time limitation into Scripture.

I believe that James 5:14-20 is for today just as it was for the first century. There are no time limitations in the text nor are there culturally limiting features. The key to the right practice is a correct interpretation of the passage.

Next question: 'Are there any theological implications that limit the text to a specific period of time?' The fact that 1 Timothy 2:15 appeals to childbearing offers a much broader basis of application than if some point limited to the first century only had been used to support the exhortation. This alone does not prove the validity of contemporary application, but it does demand careful consideration.

As a general rule, a passage should be interpreted in the broadest sense (timewise) possible. If there is nothing specifically limiting the text, then narrowing the use is unacceptable culturalizing.

Let me illustrate with a crucial issue. Is the husband head of the home? If he is, what does that mean?

Over the past twenty-five years many writers have been asserting that 'head' in such passages as 1 Corinthians 11:3 and Ephesians 5:22-24 means 'source' rather than 'authority'. Furthermore, whatever 'authority' means in the text, they claim it was dictated by a first century, patriarchal mindset and thus is limited to first century application.

But is that true? Let's ask some key questions about the Greek text to find out. In general, what does *kephale*, translated 'head', mean? In normal Greek literature it very accept-ably meant 'first', 'prominent', or 'supreme', in addition to referring to the part of the physical body.

Was *kephalē* ever used figuratively in reference to a person's being a leader? In both secular Greek and the Old Testament (Septuagint translation), *kephalē* was used in the sense of leader or ruler. Psalm 18:43 notes, 'Thou hast placed me as head of the nations.'

Is *kephalē* ever used figuratively in the New Testament to speak of authority? In Ephesians it is used in 1:22 and 4:15 of Christ as head of the church.

Now consider Ephesians 5:22-24: 'Wives, be subject to your own husbands, as to the Lord. For the husband is the head of the wife, as Christ also is the head of the church, He Himself being the Saviour of the body. But as the church is subject to Christ, so also the wives ought to be to their husbands in everything.'

Paul is drawing two conclusions by analogy. First, 'as the church is to the Lord so also the wife is to be to her husband.' Second, 'as Christ is head of the church so also the husband is head of his wife.' There are no time limitations in the text. The theological context extends beyond the first century since it focuses upon the church, which is not limited.

Therefore, we can conclude that there is nothing in the text or context that limits the passage to a particular period of history. Nor is there a modified understanding of *kephalē* so that it means less today than it did in Paul's day.

So the husband is the head of his home today just as in the first century. As Christ is the final, God-ordained head of the church, so the husband is the God-appointed head over his household.

Let me hasten to say that 'head' is not to be equated with 'dictator.' Husbands are to express their leadership by loving their wives, not lording it over them. As Christ gave Himself for the church, so husbands are to give (not take) themselves for that which benefits their wives.

Headship also does not mean 'superior' or 'better' or 'smarter.' Dr. Homer Kent spells it out correctly in *Ephesians: The Glory of the Church*: 'Wives may be the equal of and many times superior to their husbands in intelligence, courage, spirituality, moral discernment, discretion, and in a thousand other ways. Furthermore, as members of the body of Christ they are equal (Gal. 3:28). But in the matter of authority and position in the home, the Bible is absolutely clear: the wife is subject to the authority of the husband.'

Headship does mean that husbands are to live out their God-assigned role in the home. They are to be spiritual leaders of their families, not because of male superiority but in obedience to God's biblical blueprint for marriage.

One other contemporary issue deserves mention. It focuses on the recent 'inclusive language' lectionary distributed by the National Council of Churches.

Our focus centers primarily on the terms used to describe God. With the advent of 'liberation' and the demand for equality, some are saying that today's enlightened thinking demands God be understood as both male and female, father and mother. The upshot of the matter is that the NCC and others believe we need to alter the Bible to catch up with this twentieth-century thinking.

It is to be hoped that everyone can agree at the outset that God's eternal being is spirit not flesh (John 4:24). However, in God's revelation of Himself in the written Word and the living Word, it is in terms we can understand, namely, earthly terms. God accommodates Himself in the language of the Bible so that we can understand who He is by association with the things we know of from our human existence.

I suggest that to call God 'Mother' is to culturize Scripture. There are several good reasons for saying this.

1. The grammatical gender of 'God' in both the Old Testament (Elohim) and New (Theos) is masculine, not feminine.
2. Jesus always referred to the first person of the triune Godhead as Father – never as Mother.
3. When God clothed Himself in human flesh, it was with male flesh, not female flesh. This is confirmed by the fact that Jesus was circumcised on the eighth day (Luke 2:21).

God does not need a sexist-oriented, sex-crazed society to modernize His character. To do so is to culturalize away the Bible.

Now, before we leave culturalizing, let us briefly consider the flip side of the issue. That is, extending a practice into our time which in fact could have been cultural and maybe not intended by God to be practised today.

What about 'lifting hands' towards heaven as a part of worship? That is frequently mentioned in the Old Testament (Job 11:13; Pss. 28:2; 63:4; 88:9; 134:2; 141:2; 143:6; Lam. 2:19). But is it for today?

Nowhere in the New Testament is it practised by the church. The only place it really is mentioned in a church context is 1 Timothy 2:8. There is little 'time' evidence in the text to help us, except to say that if we believe it is transcultural, then it is to be done by men only, and it is limited to times of prayer alone. Note that the Old

Testament expression also encompassed times of praise, whereas Paul limits it to prayer.

If someone believes that Scripture encourages raised hands today then he must answer two key questions before he practises what he believes.

1. Are my hands holy?
2. Am I taking other people's attention away from the Lord to myself by doing something that is not practised by everyone in the service?

Whatever one decides, it must be insisted that an outward expression like raised hands never has been a mark of spirituality, for true spirituality is always measured by the attitude behind the act.

Another puzzling practice is 'the holy kiss'. It is commanded five times in the New Testament (Rom. 16:16; 1 Cor. 16:20; 2 Cor. 13:12; 1 Thess. 5:26; 1 Peter 5:14). Is it for today?

It certainly was part of first century church life and commanded by the apostles. We do know that a kissing embrace was a part of the first century culture. The added emphasis on 'holy' obviously signifies that the practice had been abused and thus there were also 'unholy' kisses. Let me suggest that the emphasis seems to be on 'greet one another'. If you believe you need to kiss, make it 'holy'. However, the common greeting in our day is a handshake or hug. If Paul were writing today, he might have commanded, 'Greet one another with either a holy hug or a holy handshake.'

The doctrine of inerrancy demands that our lives be continuously edited and revised. One author poignantly observes: 'God doesn't want our success; He wants us. He doesn't demand our achievements, He demands our obedience.'

Dare we do anything less with God's inerrant Word than 'cut it straight' and then 'toe the line'?

Questions for Discussion

1. Why must we avoid the error of *accommodation?*

2. Name some areas in which we find biblical accommodation applied today.

3. How may we protect ourselves from falling prey to accommodation?

4. When are we guilty of *culturalizing?*

5. To avoid the hazard of culturalizing a passage, what questions may we ask ourselves as we handle Scripture?

6. Examine 1 Corinthians 11:3 and Ephesians 5:22-24. What is the proper interpretation of those passages?

Ten

Twisting Scripture

Precision. It's essential in landing a 747 aircraft or performing open heart surgery. Without minute attention to detail, hundreds of passengers might die, or a patient would not make it through the operation.

Maybe you've heard of the person who carelessly opened a Bible and randomly put his finger down at, 'He went away and hanged himself' (Matt. 27:5). He didn't particularly like the message so he haphazardly tried again. This time he found, 'Go and do the same' (Luke 10:37). In frustration, he quickly made one more wild effort, which yielded, 'What you do, do quickly' (John 13:27). Carelessness in this case would lead to death.

Precision. There is no substitute.

Similarly, nothing less should be the standard for interpreting the Bible and discerning the biblical guidelines to direct our spiritual lives. That's why Paul wrote to Timothy, 'Be diligent to present yourself approved to God as a workman who does not need to be ashamed, handling accurately the word of truth' (2 Tim. 2:15). To be less than precise is literally to misrepresent the mind of God.

We continue our studies, which warn about the most common errors that Christians make in interpreting the Bible. Armed with this and some positive tips on how to 'cut it straight,' you'll be better equipped to practise precision when you come to God's Word. The errors we'll look at this time are redefining, anglizing, and mysticizing.

Redefining

I once heard of two men in a car who stopped at a major intersection. The driver asked his passenger, 'Anything coming your way?' The reply came, 'Nothing but a dog.' Seconds later there was a violent collision, and both ended up in hospital. After they regained consciousness, the driver angrily quizzed his passenger. 'I thought you said nothing but a dog was coming! What happened?'

'That's right, man,' he shot back. 'Nothing but a Grey-hound', which is the name of an American coachline company.

One word made all the difference. Well-defined words are important to good communication. Redefining is the error of giving historically accepted biblical words new definitions to support a person's theology.

I call it the 'Humpty Dumpty approach' to biblical study. Lewis Carroll put these words on the lips of his famous egg in *Through the Looking Glass*: 'When I use a word, it means just what I choose it to mean – neither more nor less!'

If we did that with words – if we changed their accepted meaning to suit our fancy – we could never communicate with one another. Similarly, God is not playing games with us. His inspired writers used words with established meanings that can be clearly understood in the context of the Bible. Thus, we can apply God's wisdom to contemporary issues.

Take the issue of abortion for instance. The key question asks, 'When does personhood begin?' A number of biblical evidences point to personhood's beginning at conception, unless, of course, one resorts to redefining.

First, the Bible does not make a definitional distinction between a child in the womb and a child after birth. The words used in the Bible do not differentiate between the two.

Exodus 21:4 and 21:22 are good examples. *Yeled*, the Hebrew word for 'child', refers to postnatal life in 21:4, yet it also translates 'a woman with child' in 21:22, referring to prenatal existence.

John the Baptist is referred to as a child (*brephos*; Luke 1:41,44) in his prenatal period. The infants slaughtered by Pharaoh after their birth (Acts 7:19) are mentioned with the same term.

Thus, both the Hebrew and the Greek cultures understood personhood to exist prior to birth.

Second, conception is the generating agent of depravity, and depravity is a chief mark of personhood. Therefore, personhood begins at conception. David declared, 'In sin my mother conceived me' (Ps. 51:5). Ephesians 2:3 affirms that persons are by nature children of wrath. Accordingly, persons then exist from conception.

Third, Moses reasoned that 'life taken' should be paid for by 'life given' if an infant in the womb died due to injury sustained by the mother (Exod. 21:22-23). The principle of 'life for life' could only be imposed if the unborn child was a person.

Finally, one of the creation mandates is that 'kind multiply after its own kind' (Gen. 1:24-25). It would be contradictory to suggest that a person procreates a nonperson. Consistency demands that a person beget a person. Thus, personhood logically begins at conception.

There are those Christians, however, who continue to define personhood as beginning sometime after conception.

Personhood is thus redefined to fit one's thoughts about abortion. Actually, the Bible's definition of person should be the starting point to then determine our theology concerning abortion.

Let's look at some other prominent examples, all of which are found in Robert Schuller's *Self Esteem: The New Reformation*. Here he redefines the biblical concepts of sin, hell, and salvation.

Schuller asks, 'What do I mean by sin? Answer: Any human condition or act that robs God of glory, by stripping one of his children of their right to divine dignity' (p. 14). However, sin is variously defined in Scripture as falling short of God's glory (Rom. 3:23), unrighteousness (1 John 5:17), and lawlessness (1 John 3:4).

'And what is hell?' Schuller continues. 'It is the loss of pride that naturally follows separation from God – the ultimate and unfailing source of our soul's sense of self respect' (p. 14). Yet the Bible describes hell as a place, not a state of mind (Rev. 20:14). Also it is experienced beyond death, not in this life.

'What does it mean to be saved?' Dr. Schuller then says, 'It means to be permanently lifted from sin (psychological self abuse with all of its consequences seen above) and shame to self-esteem and its God glorifying human need-meeting, constructive, and creative consequences' (p. 99). But the Bible variously describes salvation as repentance from sin (Acts 2:38), believing the truth about Christ (Rom. 10:9), being delivered by God from the domain of darkness to the kingdom of Christ (Col. 1:13), and as those who are dead in sins being made alive with Christ (Eph. 2:1,5).

The moderator of a television panel discussion asked one of the participants, 'Are many saved under your preaching?' The participant answered, 'We don't exactly use that terminology. We don't believe people are lost. Everyone is a god, according to Jesus.'

You immediately recognize the error of prooftexting. The Scripture alluded to is John 10:34-36, in which Jesus quotes from Psalm 82:6. Jesus is using the word 'god' in the context of the passage referring to human judges, not the divine Judge. This woman totally skirted man's need for salvation by redefining 'god' outside of the context in which Jesus used it.

Another example of redefining comes with the use of '1,000 years' or 'millennium' in Revelation 20 on six occasions (20:2-7). Does it refer to a literal 1,000-year period or to a period that is indefinitely long but can't be calculated? The whole issue of premillennialism versus amillennialism or postmillennialism is dramatically affected by the answer to this question.

Let's start by acknowledging that it is commonly understood as a basic rule of hermeneutics that numbers should be accepted at face value, that is, they convey a mathematical quantity unless there is substantial evidence to warrant otherwise. This dictum for interpreting biblical numbers is generally accepted as the proper starting point.

This rule holds true throughout the Bible, including Revelation. A survey of numbers in the Apocalypse supports this. For instance, 7 churches and 7 angels in Revelation 1 refer to 7 literal churches and their messengers. Twelve tribes and 12 apostles refer to actual, historical numbers (21:12, 14). Ten days (2:10), 5 months (9:5), $1/3$ of mankind (9:15), 2 witnesses (11:3), 42 months (11:2), 1,260 days (11:3), 12 stars (12:1), 10 horns (13:1), 200 miles (14:20), 3 demons (16:13), and 5 fallen kings (17:9-10) all use numbers in their normal sense. Out of the scores of numbers in Revelation, only two (7 spirits in 1:4 and 666 in 13:18) are conclusively used in a symbolic fashion. Although this line of reasoning does not prove that 'one thousand' in Revelation 20 should be taken normally, it does put the burden of proof otherwise on those who disagree with accepting 'one thousand' as 1,000.

Not only are numbers in general to be taken normally in Revelation, but more specially is this true with numbers referring to time. In Revelation 4-20 there are at least twenty-five references to measurements of time. Only two of these demand to be understood in something other than a literal sense, and with these numbers are not employed. The 'day of their wrath' (6:17) would likely exceed twenty-four hours, and 'the hour of His judgement' (14:7) seemingly extends beyond sixty minutes. There is nothing, however, in the phrase 'one thousand years' that suggests a symbolic interpretation.

This next point is very important. Never in the Bible is 'year' used with a numerical adjective when it does not refer to the actual period of time that it mathematically represents. Unless evidence to the contrary can be provided, Revelation 20 is not the one exception in the entire Scripture.

Also, the number one thousand is not used elsewhere in the Bible with a symbolic sense. Job 9:3; 33:23; Psalms 50:10; 90:4; Ecclesiastes 6:6; 7:28; and 2 Peter 3:8 have been used in support of the idea that one thousand in our text is used symbolically. However, these attempts fail because in each of these texts one thousand is used in its normal sense to make a vivid point.

One thousand and its varied combinations are used frequently in both Testaments. No one questions the response to 5,000 believers (Acts 4:4), 23,000 men killed

(1 Cor. 10:8), or 7,000 killed (Rev. 11:13). Likewise, there is no exegetical reason to question the normalcy of 1,000 years in Revelation 20.

To avoid making this mistake yourself or being misdirected by the error of others, here are a couple of easy steps to protect yourself.

1. Use a good concordance (Young's, Strong's, NASB Exhaustive Concordance) to trace the biblical use of a word.
2. If you have abilities in the original languages (Hebrew, Aramaic, and Greek) consult a good lexicon to see the various meanings of a word.
3. Always define a word by the context in which it is used. When a word can be used in several different ways, the specific meaning of a word in a text will be determined by the context. For example, the Hebrew word translated 'to know' can mean to know socially (Gen. 29:5) or to know sexually (Gen. 4:1). Context dictates which definition is correct.

Anglicizing

Often we can go far afield by failing to consult the original language in which God gave His Word. Inaccurate conclusions are reached by drawing theology from the English text alone. That is *anglicizing*, and it makes Webster, not God, the final authority on word meaning.

A lady once wrote me a very angry letter because a staff member at our church told her teenage daughter that she needed to become a Christian according to the Bible. This woman went on to tell me in the letter that according to Webster's dictionary, a Christian is one who believes that Jesus is the Son of God.

She related how her daughter's upbringing had taught her that truth and therefore it was an insult to insinuate her daughter wasn't a Christian. This is tragic because the lady was half right, but Webster did not take it far enough. The woman should have consulted the Bible. Intellectual belief alone is not enough (James 2:19), but one must also personally receive by faith Christ as Saviour and Lord (John 1:12-13; Rom. 10:9-13) to become a Christian.

Here is another example. People argue constantly whether Christians have two natures or one nature, when, in fact, the Greek word for 'nature' (*phusis*) is never used in the New Testament to describe the character or capacity of a person. The Bible consistently describes a person in terms of 'old man' or 'new man'. Another common anglicizing error, one that has tremendous implications, is 'positive confession.' This growing movement preaches 'What you confess, you will possess.' Don Gossett, in *The Power of the Positive Confession of God's Word*, writes, 'Our words are the coins in the Kingdom of faith' (p. 27).

Their supposed biblical basis for 'positive confession' is Hebrews 4:14: 'Since then we have a great high priest who has passed through the heavens, Jesus the Son of God, let us hold fast our confession.' They conclude from the English word confess that if we repeat, or confess, what the Bible says, then God is obliged to give to us what we confess, whether it be wealth, health, or happiness.

To teach 'positive confession' based on Hebrews 4:14 is to make the English word *confess* mean more than the Greek words (*homologeō, homolegia*). In Greek, *confession* basically means to 'say the same thing' or 'agree'. Confession is not a magical verbal trick we use to make God give us the earthly desires of our hearts.

Note carefully also that the confession of Hebrews 4:14 is our confession of faith in Christ (cf. Romans 10:9). Next observe that Hebrews 4:14, in context, is not talking about God as the provider of this world's goods but rather the giver of spiritual goods like grace and mercy in our time of need.

Jesus put it this way in Matthew 6:33: 'But seek first His kingdom and His righteousness; and all these things shall be added to you.' We are to seek the spiritual realm of life and let God administer the earthly.

In the above analysis of 'positive confession' as supposedly taught in Hebrews 4:14, we have worked through the right steps in analyzing a biblical interpretation. Let me now state them.

1. Study the word first in the original language to avoid building theology on the English translation.
2. Determine what the word specifically refers to in the text under consideration.
3. Look at the word in the broader context of its paragraph or chapter.

Mysticizing

The desire to find hidden meanings in Scripture that can be understood only by the one who knows the 'secret code' is rapidly resurfacing in evangelicalism. *Mysticizing* involves numerical codes supposedly hidden in the words of Scripture or hidden verbal meanings extracted from the words and sentences that are not to be understood in a normal, literary sense.

Hidden numerics, or gematria, as the ancients called it, is on the rise. This has recently been popularized by Jerry Lucas and Del Washburn in *Theomatics: God's Best Kept Secret*

Revealed. They seek to authenticate the Bible by showing the logic of the supposed numerical values of the alphabet.

But as John J. Davis points out in *Biblical Numerology*: 'This whole system is based on a false premise. There is no proof that the Hebrews of the Old Testament used their alphabet in this manner' (p. 149). Davis adds that gematria does nothing to improve our understanding of Scripture and only complicates the simplicity of God's Word.

Another employment of numbers used to interpret the Bible flows out of computer analysis of Scripture. One computer executive, who as a hobby seriously studies the Bible with computers, concluded about Revelation, 'The entire book is in code and every code is explained in Scripture . . . The book of Joshua is a structural model of Revelation.'

If this were true, it means that until the advent of computers, no one would have understood Revelation. Further, the promise of blessing for understanding and obeying in Revelation 1:3 is meaningless except to the few elite who have cracked the code with computers.

Recently I was discussing Revelation 13:18 and the identity of Antichrist based on 666. A man told me that he had numerically identified the Antichrist using the following analysis: The Latin name for Pope is Vicarius Filii Dei. If the numerical equivalents are substituted for the Latin letters, their sum is 666.

Our point here is not to identify Antichrist but rather to say that this mystical interpretation of 666 using Latin letters and their numerical equivalents is tenuous at best. You can make just about anyone the Antichrist by using 666 as their identity if you arbitrarily choose the right language and numerical system to work from.

I do not believe the identity of Antichrist can be proved from the number 666 by assigning numerical values to any set of letters. Six in the Bible symbolically portrays humanity, or humanness. When three sixes are put together, I believe it's God's way of emphasizing the utter humanity of the Antichrist. Just as God emphasizes His holiness by the cry of 'Holy, Holy, Holy' from the angels, so He emphasizes the humanity of Antichrist by the number six, six, six.

Probably the most common expression of mysticizing occurs in private or home Bible study. It normally is introduced with, 'This verse means to me ...' We have all had this experience. A particular passage strikes a chord in our thinking or experience and thus we believe God has hidden this in the text, even though what it means to us might contradict what has been the normal understanding of the passage since the apostles. Some even go so far as to say, 'I think I am the first person to ever see this.' If you think or hear something like it – be warned about mysticizing.

Another spin-off of this error is the so-called *rhēma* from God. Much has been made by some of the charismatic persuasion of the difference between the two Greek words for 'word' – *logos* and *rhēma*.

A *rhēma*, according to them, is usually a word from God that supposedly gives them an insight or application into the passage (*logos*) which no one would get by a normal means of interpretation.

However, there is no biblical basis for this kind of experience in Scripture. Here are two reasons:

1. *Rhēma* and *logos* are used interchangeably in the Greek translation of the Old Testament to speak about the same Hebrew word (Exod. 34:27; 1 Kings 12:24).

2. They are used interchangeably in the New Testament
   also (compare Luke 20:20 with 20:26; Acts 2:14 with
   2:22; Acts 10:36 with 10:37; 1 Pet. 1:23 with 1:25).

Let me conclude this portion with one more example, which takes a little different form. In debates about biblical issues, I always try to first establish the absolute authority of Scripture as the complete Word of God. Once a man responded by saying that in his tradition they believed that the Bible does not contain the 'words of God' but rather communicated 'the word of God.'

He was saying in effect, 'The Bible is partly from God and partly from man. Part of it is authoritative, while another part is nothing more than human opinion. We need to accept its overriding message, but it is not necessary to believe all that the Bible contains.'This man and others like him (in neo-orthodox tradition) believe they have the ability to separate the wheat from the chaff. There is some supposed mystical sense that points to truth and rejects error.

Dr. Martyn Lloyd-Jones, in his excellent book *Authority*, asks a series of pertinent questions:

Who decides what is true? Who decides what is of value? How can you discriminate between the great facts which are true and those that are false? How can you differentiate between the facts and the teaching? How can you separate this essential message of the Bible from the background in which it is presented? [5]

They can only answer, 'God's Spirit.' But we respond, 'How do you know it was God's Spirit and not your human spirit or some other spirit?' The nonsense of this approach becomes obvious when two of them come to two different conclusions concerning whether a portion of Scripture is from God or man and both use God's Spirit as their point of authority.

Be warned, this is one of the most subtle ways to make Scripture subject to the human will rather than, as it ought to be, the human mind and will being subjected to the authority of Scripture.

The Bible is a book from God that communicates truth with words, sentences, and paragraphs. Language is used by God in its normal sense, which includes literary figures of speech.

Each text has one primary interpretation, or meaning intended by God. Our task is to first draw out the correct interpretation, and then we can advance the many right applications.

By doing this you will rightly divide God's Word with precision!

Questions for Discussion

1. Describe the error of *redefining*.

2. How do some redefine Scripture with relation to the abortion issue? In what ways do they mishandle Scripture?

3. How can we avoid redefining Scripture?

4. Define *anglicizing*. What principle might we use to protect us from anglicizing the Word of God?

5. How does *mysticizing* work? Where does it most often occur?

Eleven

Over Literalizing

'REDSKINS SCALP Raiders!' Someone reading this headline out of context might conclude it refers to a bunch of irate Indians who viciously defended themselves against a band of marauding barbarians.

We know better. Given the context of sports, it describes how the Washington Redskins NFL football team scored a lopsided victory over the Oakland Raiders.

Newspapers require their readers to use basic rules of interpretation in order to understand what they mean. So does the Bible.

Use this basic rule of thumb. Interpret the Bible normally, like any piece of literature, whilst allowing for figures of speech and special kinds of literature such as poetic or prophetic.

Now we'll see how the overliteralization of this basic rule can result in misinterpreting the Bible.

Letterism

Jesus said, 'I am the bread of life' (John 6:48) and, 'I am the door' (John 10:9). Did He really mean He was actually a loaf of bread and actually the gate to an earthly sheepfold?

We quickly answer no, unless we are taken in by *letterism*. Ignoring figures of speech and drawing woodenly literal conclusions can lead to serious error.

Several years ago a man sat in my office and tried to explain what Jesus meant in John 6:53 when He said, 'Truly, truly, I say to you, unless you eat the flesh of the Son of Man and drink His blood, you have no life in yourselves.' He kept telling me it meant what it said but he would not explain the text. So I finally asked him, 'If you had lived back then and stood in Christ's presence when He spoke those words, how would you have responded? Like the Pharisees who did not understand how Christ could literally offer His flesh? (6:52); or the disciples who found the statement difficult and departed (6:60, 66)?' He finally confessed that he would have run up to Christ and requested an actual bite out of His hand.

While this might sound extreme, it is the very logical end of letterism. The failure to recognize that Jesus was using a metaphor (the declaration that one thing is another) resulted in this man's sincere but very wrong interpretation.

A man recently stopped by a table where my wife and I were having lunch to ask a theological question. He wondered, 'If soul sleep follows death, when do we actually see the Lord?'

He undoubtedly had read some cultic literature that speaks of soul sleep, which is erroneously supported by such passages as John 11:11: 'This He said, and after that He said to them, 'Our friend Lazarus has fallen asleep; but I go, that I may awaken him out of sleep.'' And 1 Thessalonians 4:13, 'But we do not want you to be uninformed, brethren, about those who are asleep, that you may not grieve, as do the rest who have no hope.'

Both verses speak of death using the term *sleep* euphemistically. The more pleasant term *sleep* is used in place of *dead* because it does not sound as offensive. Dead people outwardly appear to sleep when in fact they are really dead. It is a more pleasant way of describing someone who is dead. Even the disciples missed this at first. 'The disciples therefore said to Him, "Lord, if he has fallen asleep, he will recover." Now Jesus had spoken of his death, but they thought that He was speaking of literal sleep' (John 11:12-13). But Jesus set them straight, 'Then Jesus therefore said to them plainly, 'Lazarus is dead" (11:14).

Letterism in this instance leads to the heretical idea of the intermediate state of 'soul sleep' intervening after death but before being in the presence of God. Paul says, however, 'We are of good courage, I say, and prefer rather to be absent from the body and to be at home with the Lord' (2 Cor. 5:8). There is no 'soul sleep' stated.

Other related cultic errors involve attributing bodily parts to God and making Him less than fully God and fully spirit in being. Because the Bible speaks of God's arm (Ps. 89:21), right hand (Ps. 17:7), face (Ps. 10:11), eye (Ps. 11:4), mouth (Ps. 119:13), and nostrils (Ps. 18:8,15), some have concluded God must live in a human body.

Actually the Bible says, 'God is not a man' (Num. 23:19; cf. 1 Sam. 15:29). Attributing human features to God is a literary speech figure called *anthropomorphism*. God who is spirit (John 4:24) is spoken of in human terms so that we who are human can in a limited way understand what God is like because He is described in terms we know.

In discussing a contemporary issue once, I insisted strongly that we take the Bible literally, that is, at face value. One who disagreed tried to prove his point by asking a rather odd question, 'Have you ever sinned?' I responded in the affirmative, not quite understanding where the discussion was headed.

My opponent then demanded that if I took the Bible literally I should have cut off my hand because that is what Jesus taught. Somewhat surprised by his naive approach, I responded by asking, 'Have you never heard about figures of speech?'

What Jesus actually said was: 'And if your right eye makes you stumble, tear it out, and throw it from you; for it is better for you that one of the parts of your body perish, than for your whole body to be thrown into hell. And if your right hand makes you stumble, cut it off, and throw it from you; for it is better for you that one of the parts of your body perish, than for your whole body to go into hell' (Matt. 5:29-30). It is in the context of Christ's discussing lust and adultery. Any thinking person understands that Jesus was using hyperbole (extravagant exaggeration) to make His point about the awful consequences of lust. It is the same kind of unforgettable statement Christ makes in Matthew 19:24: 'And again I say to you, it is easier for a camel to go through the eye of a needle, than for a rich man to enter the kingdom of God.'

Imagine what letterism would lead us to believe if that's how we interpreted 2 Chronicles 16:9: 'For the eyes of the LORD move to and fro throughout the earth that He may strongly support those whose heart is completely His.' Or, 'He will cover you with His pinions, and under His wings you may seek refuge; His faithfulness is a shield and bulwark' (Ps. 91:4). God's eyes don't have legs, and God is not a bird. These are figures of speech used to make the words colourfully memorable.

These illustrations have been rather obvious, but others are more difficult. Is the white horse of Revelation 19:11 an actual horse kept in heaven, or does it symbolically picture the reality of Christ's victorious return to earth? Is the 'lake of fire' in Revelation 20:14-15 real fire, or is it a graphic impression to describe the kind of incredibly painful experience of actual hell? Will blood literally be up to the horses' bridles over a land mass of 200 miles (Rev. 14:20), or does this unforgettably picture the tremendous human toll because of God's wrath?

With more than 250 distinctly different kinds of speech figures used in the Bible, how can we ever be sure of one interpretation? Here are some simple steps that will help:

1. Begin with the basic principle that the Bible is to be interpreted normally.
2. Familiarize yourself with the kinds of figures used in the Bible. *Figures of Speech Used in the Bible* by E.W. Bullinger is the best tool to have for handy reference in your library.
3. Remember that every symbol or figure represents an actual truth or reality. Ask yourself what it could possibly be.
4. Look to see if the broader text identifies and interprets the symbol for you, in the way Revelation 1:20 identifies the reality of the seven lampstands (1:13) and the seven stars (1:16) as seven actual churches and seven actual messengers.
5. If your text does not interpret the figure, see if it is a figure used and interpreted elsewhere in Scripture.
6. Finally, remember that some figures of speech are incapable of dogmatic interpretation (many parables, for example) and thus should never be the basis for doctrine.

Legalizing

Letterism is an error of interpretation. *Legalizing* is actually a mistake that involves both interpretation and application. It involves overemphasizing the letter of God's Word at the expense of its spirit (2 Cor. 3:6). The entire book of Malachi was written to a people and priesthood who had legalized away the true heart of worship. They went through the motions of outward form, but their heart was never in it. They mocked God by their self-centered, self-approved activities.

The Pharisees gave alms (Matt. 6:2-4), prayed (6:5), and fasted (6:16-18) but without eternal reward. Their activities impressed men who looked on the outside but not God who examines the heart: 'But the LORD said to Samuel, "Do not look at his appearance or at the height of his stature, because I have rejected him; for God sees not as man sees, for man looks at the outward appearance, but the LORD looks at the heart" '(1 Sam. 16:7).

One day Samuel shocked Saul with this amazing statement: 'Has the LORD as much delight in burnt offerings and sacrifices as in obeying the voice of the LORD? Behold, to obey is better than sacrifice, and to heed than the fat of rams' (1 Sam. 15:22; see also Micah 6:6-8). God is far more interested in the motives behind obedience than He is in the form.

Some today would measure acceptable or non-acceptable worship by the types of musical instruments included or excluded. In the 60s and 70s guitars were not acceptable in many churches. On the other hand, some churches thought if you didn't use guitars your praise was inferior. The truth of the matter is that you can worship God with a symphonic diversity of instruments (Ps. 150) or without instruments

(Eph. 5:19-20). The type of instrument has nothing to do with true worship. Why you play, what you play, and how you play are more important.

In Los Angeles there is a home church movement. Its proponents believe it is more spiritual to worship in houses than in church buildings. For them it is a major issue, and they cite the pattern of the first century church's meeting in homes (Acts 2:46; 5:42; 12:12; 20:20; Rom. 16:5; 1 Cor. 16:19; Col. 4:15; Philem. 2; 2 John 10).

Actually, homes are acceptable places to gather. But there are other equally acceptable locations such as hills (Luke 6:12,17), seashores (Matt. 13:1-2), riversides (Acts 16:13), and public buildings (Acts 3:1). Nowhere in the Bible is there is a list of unacceptable places.

One of the most serious errors of legalism centers on the version of the Bible you use. For example, some condemn anyone who dares to suggest that a version other than the King James Version is reliably the Word of God. For 'KJV only' advocates, the only two reliable Bibles ever given by God are the original manuscripts written by the prophets and apostles and the 1611 translation we call the King James Version.

Whole movements and schools have made the King James Version the cornerstone of their existence. They offer complicated arguments for the superiority of the 1611 translation, which was made from relatively late manuscripts. Most evangelical scholars agree that over centuries of copying, many minor errors had crept into those texts. Since 1611, a large number of much older manuscripts have become available, and translators have learned more about ancient Greek and Hebrew. For further reading, let me suggest *The King James Version Debate* by D.A. Carson.

There is no necessary connection between the adoption of the King James Version and the inspiration of Scripture. There are equally godly, scholarly men on both sides of this issue who all strongly embrace the historic, orthodox understanding of the inerrancy and infallibility of the Scriptures.

Adoption of the *King James Version* should never be made a point of theological orthodoxy or ecclesiastical fellowship. A believer should continue to use an accurate English translation that is personally most readable and understandable such as the *King James Version, New American Standard Bible*, or *English Standard Version.*

Several guidelines will keep you off this spiritual detour:

1. Be careful of legalizing to distinguish between the desired end and the means to the end. Is the place we worship the end of worship or just the means? If it is the means, then don't make it the end. To do so is legalizing.
2. Distinguish between outward form and inward motive. Ask, 'Why am I doing this?' Make sure your motives are pure and your attention directed Godward, not toward man.
3. Distinguish between observance and expression that are absolute and those that are cultural. If it's absolute, everyone ought to adopt it. If it is cultural and not now biblically forbidden or impossible, then it might be good for you, but don't make it a mark of true spirituality for everyone else.

Worship in homes or outside of homes, music with or without a guitar, King James Bible or other legitimate translations are up to personal preference. Never should they be used as a test for Christian fellowship.

Role of prayer

When a text is tough, I take the advice once given to a man of another generation: H.A. Ironside told of visiting an Irishman, Andrew Frazer, who had come to Southern California to recover from a serious illness. Though quite weak, he opened his worn Bible and began expounding the deep truths of God in a way that Ironside had never heard before.

Ironside was so moved by Frazer's words that he asked him, 'Where did you get these things? Could you tell me where I could find a book that would open them up to me? Did you learn them in some seminary or college?' The sickly man gave an answer that Ironside said he would never forget. 'My dear young man, I learned these things on my knees on the mud floor of a little sod cottage in the north of Ireland. There with my open Bible before me I used to kneel for hours at a time and ask the Spirit of God to reveal Christ to my soul and to open the Word to my heart. He taught me more on my knees on that mud floor than I ever could have learned in all the seminaries or colleges in the world.'

The next time a tough text comes your way, close your eyes and kneel in prayer. Then 'cut it straight!'

Questions for Discussion

1. List some basic rules of literary interpretation generally adhered to. Do those basic rules also apply to biblical interpretation?

2. What is the error of *letterism*? Cite some examples you have heard of letterism dealing with the text of Scripture.

3. Name steps we can take to properly interpret figures of speech in the Bible.

4. Describe *legalism*. How does it differ from *letterism*?

5. Why is it wrong to condemn the use of a Bible version because it is not the version we prefer to use? How should we deal with this kind of legalism?

Twelve

Reverse Interpretation

I MAGINE THE thrill of receiving a first love letter. Excitedly ripping into this special message, you read, 'I love you.'

In all the exhilaration, there are three possible ways to understand those magic words: (1) In terms of what you want the letter to say, which might be, 'Will you marry me?' Or (2) what you think the writer meant to say, such as, 'I love you more than I have ever loved anyone,' or (3) a more realistic approach, which is to believe that it means what it says, simply, 'I love you.'

The Bible is God's love letter to humanity. Many have tried to make it say what they wanted it to say. Others have read between the lines only to miss what God really intended. To get it right, we continue 'cutting it straight' in order to understand God's message of love.

Generalizing

One of today's great threats to a correct interpretation of the Bible is assuming that any specific historical experience reported in Scripture is a valid, general experience for today. This line of thinking is normally based on such passages as Malachi 3:6: 'For I, the LORD, do not change,' or Hebrews 13:8: 'Jesus Christ is the same yesterday and today, yes and forever.'

The danger was emphasized to me recently when I visited the University of California at Los Angeles (UCLA) campus as one of three panellists discussing the charismatic movement. Each participant had been asked to 'present his viewpoint and show his biblical support'.

The first person said he believed that charismatic phenomena should be considered normative today because they were normative in the apostolic church. He showed from the early chapters in Acts that charismatic experiences were not unusual.

A different approach marked the next panellist. He reasoned that if God had done something in the past, then we should not deny that He could do it today. However, he did admit that tongues and other such experiences were not for everyone today.

In both instances, they based their thinking on the idea that what God has done in the past we can automatically expect that God will do again.

When my time came, I discussed several biblical truths. First, God's ability to do something is not the real issue. God is able to do all things, at all times, in any way He chooses. But rather, God's will to act is the determining factor. Jeremiah 32:17 asserts, 'Nothing is too difficult for Thee.' And yet God cannot lie (Titus 1:2), or deny Himself (2 Tim. 2:13), or be tempted (James 1:13), or flood the whole earth again (Gen. 9:11).

God cannot lie because that would contradict His true nature. He cannot be tempted because that would violate His righteous character. He cannot deny Himself because that would contradict His eternal existence. He cannot flood the world because that would contradict His revealed will.

Second, I pointed out that it is wrong to reason that because God has done a certain thing in the past, He will automatically do it for you or others. Don't let anyone send you on a guilt trip by convincing you that to say God is not doing something today is to deny God or to make God less than God. Unless we can show by the authority of Scripture that it is God's will to do something, then to say He can and demand that He perform is to sinfully presume on God.

Third, I pointed out that God has always warned about the counterfeit – false prophets (Deut. 13:1-5; 18:14-22), false apostles (2 Cor. 12:12), and even false believers (Matt. 7:13-23). Jesus warned that neither exclamations such as 'Lord, Lord' nor experiences like miracles or exorcisms necessarily distinguished between the true and false (Matt. 7:21-23). Thus, to *generalize* is to open wide the gate for all sorts of error and deception.

Many today claim to be ministering on God's behalf, with God's message and power. They authenticate their ministry by the fact that they are doing today what the prophets or Christ or the apostles did earlier.

Don't unquestioningly accept their assertions. Check out their ministry with Scripture and see if it is God's will to be doing through men what they are doing. Also check out the message they preach to see if it squares with what the Bible really teaches. And check out their lives to see if they are being lived in conformity with the message they preach.

Let me illustrate. Some time ago national media focused attention on the late Dr. Hobart Freeman and his Faith Assembly in north-central Indiana. Freeman taught that Christians should look to God for healing as in the days of Christ. He also insisted that using doctors and medicine demonstrates a lack of faith in God. These assertions cannot be supported scripturally.

Over a decade scores of people in that congregation died, most of them children or pregnant women. Several couples were indicted because proper medical attention was allegedly withheld from the deceased, which led to their deaths. This is one example of the tragic results that come from generalizing. Dr. Freeman's own death undermined the credibility of his teaching.

If generalizing were applied broadly to all biblical experiences, we would come to some rather obvious wrong conclusions. Because a few people were raised from the dead in the past, we would believe that God raises people today. Or because God supernaturally supplied food to the Jews in the wilderness (Exod. 16:1-21) and prevented their clothes and shoes from wearing out during their four-decade journey in the wilderness (Deut. 29:5), God will feed and cloth us that way today.

We are not expecting a trip to the third heaven like Paul's (2 Cor. 12:1-10). Nor do we believe that God restocks the food supply of those who feed travelling preachers as He did for the widow of Zarephath in 1 Kings 17:8-16. Leprosy patients do not dip seven times in a river to be cured (2 Kings 5:1-14). Nor do we throw sticks on the ground and expect them to turn into serpents (Exod. 4:2-3).

Because generalizing can lead to such mistaken conclusions, what can we do to avoid it?

1. Acknowledge the danger of generalizing and remind yourself of it every time you study the Bible.
2. Study your Scripture text in its historical context to determine exactly what happened and why.
3. Look at the rest of the Bible to see if the same kind of experience is repeated frequently, infrequently, or never again.

4. Ask if there are other teaching texts in the Bible that indicate the experience or situation is normative and should be expected today.

5. Finally, double-check to make sure you have correctly distinguished between God's ability to do again something that He has done in the past and God's will to do it today.

Let me drive home the error of *generalizing* with a scriptural illustration before we move on to *experientializing*. Paul's healing ministry was spectacular. 'And God was performing extraordinary miracles by the hands of Paul, so that handkerchiefs or aprons were even carried from his body to the sick, and the diseases left them and the evil spirits went out' (Acts 19:11-12). Yet later on in his ministry he could not heal Epaphroditus (Phil. 2:25), he left Trophimus sick at Miletus (2 Tim. 4:20), and he told Timothy to take a little wine for his stomach problem (1 Tim. 5:23). Paul himself had a severe eye problem, which he could not heal (Gal. 4:12-15), and he finally died (2 Tim. 4:6), unable to cure himself. Paul ministered according to God's will, not according to God's ability to act or what God had done previously in his life.

Experientializing

Another obstacle to good Bible interpretation, *experientializing*, begins with personal experience. It reasons that if any experience has occurred in Scripture, and I have the same experience, then it must be from God.

The line of thinking uses experience to validate Scripture rather than vice versa. But that is not the proper way to approach experience.

We need to begin with the Bible to see if the experience could possibly be from God. Remember that there were those who claimed their tongue-speaking was from God. Yet Paul said no one with the Spirit of God could say what some of the Corinthians were saying – that Jesus is accursed (1 Cor. 12:3). In other words, God's Spirit was not the source of their tongues-speaking.

If the experience could come from God, then it needs to be tested by Scripture and other godly people. Jesus taught that fruit would be the test (Matt. 7:20). Paul said that prophets were to be tested by prophets (1 Cor. 14:29) and that all things were to be tested whether they be good or evil (1 Thess. 5:21). John made it very clear when he warned about false prophets and commanded believers to test them and see if they were from God (1 John 4:1).

If we read experience back into the Bible rather than beginning with Scripture to evaluate the experience, we may end in great confusion.

A man I recently read about became involved in charismatic renewal as a teen but later went on to study the Bible at non-charismatically-oriented schools. After all of this he concluded, 'I came to regard myself as an evangelical in theology and a charismatic in experience.' His tension is that he cannot support the charismatic experience from Scripture, but he can testify to the reality of the experience.

He fails in his thinking to accept the logical conclusion that if the experience cannot be supported by Scripture, then it did not come from God. It could have been self-generated, or it could even have come from Satan. Also, the account of the experience could be second hand and thus misrepresented or misunderstood.

Oftentimes an alleged healing is supported by people because of a misleading report. That is, the sincerely given report just does not match the facts as they occurred. A vivid illustration of that was provided by George Peters, former professor of missions at Dallas Theological Seminary. Having heard many stories of healings from the Indonesian revival (written about by Mel Tari in *A Mighty Wind*), Peters decided to go to Indonesia to interview people and find out first-hand what had happened.

He talked to people who were 'raised from the dead' and questioned those who had been healed. His findings were published in the book *Indonesian Revival*. One portion of what he wrote deals with people who were raised from the dead. He reports:

> The reports from Timor that God raised some people from the dead have startled many American Christians. I do not doubt that God is able to raise the dead, but I seriously question that He did so in Timor. In fact, I am convinced that it did not happen . . .
>
> I visited a man who is known in the community as having been raised from the dead. I met a woman who reported that her infant daughter of four months had been raised. I talked to the woman who was said to be responsible for having brought back to life two people, and to the man who claimed to have been instrumental in raising two people from the dead, a boy of twelve and a man forty to forty-five years old.
>
> In my questioning, I kept the sentiments of the people in mind. Their absolutist beliefs will not respond to questions of doubt. I was also aware of the fact that their word for death may mean unconsciousness, coma, or actual death. I also knew of their traditional belief in the journey of the soul after death from the body to the land of their ancestors.
>
> I had to explore the experiences of these people while they were in the state of death, how far they had 'travelled,' so to speak, between death and resuscitation. It became

apparent that death takes place in three stages, according to their beliefs. In the first stage, the soul is still in the body; in the second stage, the soul may be in the home or immediate community; and in the third stage, the soul takes its flight to the beyond and the land of the ancestors. Not one of the dead persons believed his soul had completely departed to the region beyond. That is the region of no return . . .

One man told me that his soul had been so near his body during his state of death that he was able to hear people come near to his body. However, he was not able to speak or move. He was able to relate experiences during his state of death. After some questioning, his wife added, 'My husband was not absolutely and totally dead' . . . The mother whose infant daughter was raised was quite sure that her soul had not left her body, for she had been dead only about half an hour. An older man was able to describe his condition after dying. While dead he had promised God that if he could ever live again he would confess his sins and pay back the money that he had stolen from an evangelist. He was sure that this theft had caused his sudden death, and so was the evangelist who brought him back to life . . .

I shall leave my judgements about these miracles to the reader. I went away satisfied that according to their usage of the word death, and their concept of death, they had experienced resuscitation. According to my concept of death, no such miracles happened; I learned again the value of seeing words and concepts from the people's point of view and interpreting them according to their mentality and understanding. [6]

Those people were in a state of unconsciousness or in a comatose state. They had not reached the point where their life processes were irreversibly stopped – from which point no human being can return unless God supernaturally intervenes.

I recall a man who was not a part of the charismatic movement but had periodically experienced the tongues phenomenon privately – both he and his wife. We talked about it, and I showed him where the Scriptures teach that tongues are for others' edification, not self (1 Cor. 14:12,26), and that tongues were for a sign to unbelievers, not believers (14:22). But he insisted that, in spite of what the Bible taught, he knew that God gave him this self-gratifying experience.

For him, tongues became a heightened level of spirituality. I showed him from the Scriptures that tongues are never mentioned as a fruit of the Spirit (Gal. 5:22-23) nor mentioned as a normal indication that we are filled with the Spirit (Eph. 5:15-21). Never is tongues used as a spiritual qualifying factor for the leadership responsibility of elder/overseer (1 Tim. 3:1-7; Titus 1:5-9). But he insisted on experientializing.

Here is another example. Homosexuals try to validate their illicit sexual experience, which seems right to them, by starting with their experience and attempting to find scriptural support for it. They come to Scripture and cannot find biblical support, so they misinterpret the Bible.

As mentioned earlier, they resort to prooftexting, which is then combined with experientializing. Instead of recognizing that passages such as Leviticus 18:22; 20:13; Romans 1:26-27; 1 Corinthians 6:9-11; and 1 Timothy 1:10 prohibit homosexuality, they assert that these texts support it. They also argue that David and Jonathan, as well as John and Jesus, had homosexual relationships, and therefore those kind of relationships are valid today. In fact, these men were not homosexual but rather experienced a nonsexual, pure relationship.

How can we avoid experientializing? To begin with, don't seek the spectacular, especially when you are sensing a lack of spiritual vibrancy in your life. Next, make certain you are experiencing and prayerfully seeking the kinds of experiences that the Bible marks out as normal for everyone: love (1 Cor. 13:1-7); the fruit of the Spirit (Gal. 5:22-23); control by the Spirit (Eph. 5:15-21); and the Beatitude attitudes (Matt. 5:3-11).

Third, never accept an experience as from God unless it can be validated by Scripture. In cases where you are unsure, be certain to check with the spiritual leader in your local church.

Some might ask, 'Why be so particular?' 'Is interpreting the Bible correctly such an important issue?' These questions demand a fair answer. And it is, 'Yes!' for when dealing with the Book of books, nothing less than our best is demanded to 'cut it straight' (2 Tim. 2:15).

Henry van Dyke eloquently describes why our interpretation of Scripture deserves excellence.

Born in the East and clothed in Oriental form and imagery, the Bible walks the way of all the world with familiar feet, and enters land after land to find its own everywhere. It has learned to speak in hundreds of languages to the heart of man. It comes into the palace to tell the monarch that he is a servant of the Most High, and into the cottage to assure the peasant that he is a son of God. Children listen to its stories with wonder and delight, and wise men ponder them as parables of life. It has a word of peace for the time of peril, a word of comfort for the time of calamity, a word of light for the hour of darkness. Its oracles are repeated in the assembly of the people, and its counsels whispered in the ear of the lonely. The wicked and the proud tremble at its warnings, but to the wounded and

the penitent it has a mother's voice. The wilderness and
the solitary place have been made glad by it, and the fire
on the hearth has lit the reading of its well-worn pages.
It has woven itself into our dearest dreams; so that love,
friendship, sympathy and devotion, memory and hope put
on the beautiful garments of its treasured speech, breathing
of frankincense and myrrh.[7]

Our chief desire should be to know the mind of God revealed
in the Word of God. Let's be honest with Scripture rather
than dishonest with ourselves and life when we discover that
Scripture does not support our expectation or experience.
Such a treasure as Scripture deserves our very best effort
in 'cutting it straight'.

Questions for Discussion

1. What do we mean by 'reverse interpretation'?

2. What is the danger of *generalizing*?

3. What steps can be taken to avoid generalizing?

4. Describe *experientializing*. What is its basic error?

5. How may we avoid experientializing?

Thirteen

Over Systematizing

I ONCE SPOKE at a university campus on the subject 'Is God Christian?' Afterward a gentleman approached me, red in the face and shaking with anger, to take issue with the biblical facts he did not care to accept.

After his heated retort, I asked myself, 'What else could I have said to persuade him of his need of a Saviour and salvation by faith in Jesus Christ alone?' Then it dawned on me that, at least for this encounter, nothing else could have been said, because his response translated, 'Don't confuse me with the facts; my mind is already made up.'

That incident reminded me anew that any of us can fall prey to the same mindset when we study Scripture. We've heard a doctrine proclaimed so many times or we have taught it so frequently that we are unwilling or see no need to go back and re-examine what we believe in light of the entire Bible.

It is healthy for Christians to know scripturally why we believe as we do. We never want to interpret Scripture by predetermined theology; rather we need to develop theology by the correct interpretation of individual passages. Their particular contributions can then be summarized in a theological statement on a certain subject or doctrine.

This time we look at two culprits that wrongly urge us to stay in our theological rut and never come up for a fresh burst of biblical light. The first of these is dogmatizing.

Dogmatizing

Logicians call dogmatizing 'circular reasoning'. Instead of starting with individual pieces of evidence and then reaching a conclusion, one starts with a conclusion, which is then used to interpret the evidence, thereby assuring that the desired conclusion will be affirmed. For the Bible student, this error occurs when he rigidly interprets Scripture by using a pre-determined doctrine or tradition. No one is immune from this dread disease regardless of his theological persuasions.

Several years ago I participated in a series of radio talk shows that examined various prophetic schools of thought. One listener called in to question another guest with the query, 'How does your system account for Daniel 9:24-27?' The man responded, 'I am not sure what those verses mean exactly, but I do know that my system is right.'

This is the classic mistake we all want to avoid. If our system or doctrine is correct, it will allow for the knowable interpretation of specific texts. It could be that a correct interpretation of Daniel 9:24-27 would have demanded his system be rewritten.

Let me be more specific by looking at the subject of 'tithing'. Many people faithfully give 10 percent because they believe the Bible teaches tithing for today. To question tithing is, in their eyes, almost to make the inquirer a heretic.

Yet several biblical facts escape their attention. First, the Mosaic concept of tithing involved $23^1/_3$ percent of one's income, not 10 percent. There was an annual tithe to the Lord (Lev. 27:20-32), plus an annual tithe for the nation (Deut. 14:22-27), in addition to an every-third-year tithe for the poor (Deut. 14:28-29).

Second, although tithe is mentioned eight times in the New Testament, it appears always in a historical context. Never is tithing commanded in the New Testament as a standard of giving for the church. Rather 'grace giving' is the norm presented to the churches in the epistles (1 Cor. 16; 2 Cor. 8–9). Whatever we give is between us and the Lord as He has prospered us (1 Cor. 16:2).

The error is made when Scripture is strained through the grid of doctrine, when instead the Bible should be the starting point and pattern by which we shape and purify our human expressions of God's truth. Pretribulationists* (of which I am one) often are so eager to prove their point that they see pretribulation in every possible text. Revelation 4:1-2 is often approached as a chief proof, and yet, when one looks at that text describing John's experience, one wonders how it teaches about the rapture at all.

Have you wondered how pretribulationists and post-tribulationists can both argue with equal intensity for their position from 1 Thessalonians 4:13-18? It is because they dogmatize, or read what they believe, into the text. Actually, this significant text clearly teaches the fact of the 'rapture' (1 Thess. 4:17, *harpazō*), but there are no definitive time indicators. The time relationship of the rapture to the tribulation must be determined from other passages.

Each side approaches the issue with a preconceived conclusion and then fits the facts to make its view sound right. In fact, they need to start fresh with prayer for God's

---

* All pretribulationists and a few posttribulationists interpret prophecy from the futuristic premillennial viewpoint. They differ as to whether or not the church will be raptured before or after the seven year Tribulation period which will occur immediately before Christ comes to reign on earth for 1,000 years. The Tribulation period is the final week of Daniel's prophecy in Daniel 9:24-27.

instruction and a desire to look at all the biblical data to the view of understanding God's mind rather than defending a dogma. It could be that there is a better description of the biblical data, which neither side is willing to admit because it would show both partially wrong.

Another classic example involves the extent of Christ's atonement. Some point to texts like: 'Even as the Father knows Me and I know the Father; and I lay down My life for the sheep' (John 10:15). 'Husbands, love your wives, just as Christ also loved the church and gave Himself up for her' (Eph. 5:25). They conclude that Christ died for His sheep and gave Himself for the church; therefore, the atonement is definitely limited.

Others point to texts such as: 'For it is for this we labor and strive, because we have fixed our hope on the living God who is the Savior of all men, especially of believers' (1 Tim. 4:10). 'And He Himself is the propitiation for our sins; and not for ours only, but also for those of the whole world' (1 John 2:2). It is concluded that Christ died for everyone although not everyone will be saved. Thus, they teach an unlimited atonement.

It is neither our purpose here to resolve the issue nor will space permit, but let me say that if one approaches the issue with dogmatism, the real truth of the matter will never be discovered.

Actually, the atonement is both limited and unlimited. Calvinists limit the atonement's effect by God's sovereignty, whereas the Arminians limit the atonement's effect by man's will. Both have to admit the atonement is limited.

Yet both sides also have to acknowledge that in some senses it is unlimited. In its value and suitability to the human race it is unlimited, not to mention that the atonement's message is to be proclaimed without limit. Dogmatism has no place in this kind of biblical study.

We are all susceptible to this problem, however, and at times will succumb to its lure. How can we guard against it? These steps will help:

1. Begin with the psalmist's prayer, 'Teach me Thy statutes' (Ps. 119:12). That way you will be more concerned with discerning the mind of God than with defending your position.
2. Emphasize the inductive approach to Bible study (start with a text and later move towards a systematized theology).
3. Test your dogma with Scripture rather than checking out Scripture with your theology.
4. Make sure you have looked at all the biblical evidence, even the tough texts that those who disagree use to prove you wrong.
5. Never be afraid of where a careful, disciplined study of Scripture will lead.
6. Always check your conclusion with godly Bible students to insure your objectivity.

Dispensationalizing

Dispensationalism is the school of theology that is commonly identified with belief in the rapture of believers before the Tribulation and Christ's second coming to introduce the 1000-year millennial age as the earthly fulfilment of the Abrahamic and Davidic Covenants.

The error of *dispensationalizing* is marked by an over-emphasis on the variations in God's stewardship of redemption throughout history and a minimizing of God's never-changing dealings with mankind according to His never-changing character.

Dispensationalists sometimes make such a dramatic distinction between law and grace that they appear to be minimizing God's authority in the law or to be saying that, until Christ's first coming, grace had not existed, when in fact God's grace and law have existed simultaneously in all of God's redeeming activities. Law existed before Moses for Adam (Gen. 2:16-17) and for Abraham (Gen. 26:5), and so did grace (Gen. 3:8-24). If God's Word is authoritative today with consequences for disobedience, then, in a broad sense, New Testament commandments are also 'law'.

Such an overemphasized distinction between law and grace has been made at times that some have accused dispensationalists of teaching two ways of salvation – salvation by law before the cross and salvation by grace after Calvary. Actually the Bible teaches that salvation has always been by God's grace apart from the law or works. All dispensationalists, if asked, would agree.

At times dispensationalists have taught that the Sermon on the Mount is not for today because it is pre-Calvary. However, everything Jesus taught that day was built upon the holy character of His righteously perfect, heavenly Father (Matt. 5:48). The demand of Christ's sublime sermon is that we think, talk, and act like God. One only need note that the behavioural imperatives of our Saviour's message are all repeated in the New Testament epistles.

In the past, certain dispensationalists distinguished between the terms 'kingdom of God' and 'kingdom of heaven'. But Matthew 19:23-24 uses the terms inter-changeably, as do Matthew and Mark in parallel accounts (Matt. 18:3; Mark 10:15). Therefore, it is better to understand heaven as metonymy, a figure of speech that uses the name of one thing for that of another with which it is associated. Rather than being two separate terms, kingdom of God and kingdom of heaven have the same intended meaning.

As a mild dispensationalist, I take this warning to heart. We should never let the dispensational system unwarrantedly color our interpretation of individual Scripture texts. The following guidelines will help us all:

1. Acknowledge that Scripture teaches a redemptive unity based on God's never-changing character and eternally determined plan of salvation.
2. While believing that there are various historical epochs of God's redeeming grace, always be asking, 'Where is the fine line that divides between diversity and unity?'
3. When a distinction is made, always double-check it with the question, 'Is this a distinction Scripture makes, or is it a contrast that my system demands?'

A final word

Let me conclude by returning to 2 Timothy 2:15: 'Be diligent to present yourself approved to God as a workman who does not need to be ashamed, handling accurately the word of truth.'

Paul is here teaching Timothy three truths about handling Scripture. First is the impeccability of God's Word, for it is 'the word of truth.' Paul proclaims, rather than defends, the inerrancy of Scripture.

From this truth Paul draws his next point. The interpreter of Scripture must be faithful and skilful as a workman committed to accurately handle Scripture. This is the responsibility of anyone who would interpret Scripture.

Finally Paul reminds Timothy of his accountability before God. One day we will all stand before the divine Author of the Book and hear His estimation of our interpretive labors.

That's why there is one thing worse than denying the doctrine of inerrancy. It is to affirm the doctrine but, being less than careful with the biblical text, to misrepresent God by preaching an errant message from His perfect Book. With strong doctrinal stands comes a heightened sense of responsibility to live up to them.

Although not everyone will agree with all of the illustrations used in this section, we can all profit by the principles laid down. They will help to guide us away from the shallow waters of interpretative errors, in which we otherwise would run aground.

Let's join the psalmist in praying:

[33]Teach me, O Lord, the way of Thy statutes,
And I shall observe it to the end.
[34]Give me understanding, that I may observe Thy law,
And keep it with all my heart.
[35]Make me walk in the path of Thy commandments,
For I delight in it.
[36]Incline my heart to Thy testimonies,
And not to dishonest gain.
[37]Turn away my eyes from looking at vanity,
And revive me in Thy ways.
[38]Establish Thy word to Thy servant,
As that which produces reverence for Thee.
[39]Turn away my reproach which I dread,
For Thine ordinances are good.
[40]Behold, I long for Thy precepts;
Revive me through Thy righteousness (Ps. 119:33-40).

Questions for Discussion

1. Define *dogmatizing*. What is the danger of this error?

2. How can we guard against dogmatizing?

3. What is *dispensationalizing*? Cite some examples from the Bible of how this error can mar the intended meaning of a passage.

4. List some guidelines we can follow that will help us avoid dispensationalizing passages in the Bible.

A SUMMARY OF 'CROOKED CUTS'

1. A Text Without a Context

A. Prooftexting: Stringing together an inappropriate or inadequate series of Bible verses to prove our theology.

B. Isolationism: Failing to interpret a single Scripture text in light of its context.

2. Adding To Scripture

A. Spiritualizing: Reading a spiritual or historical truth *into* a text rather than extracting truth *from* it.

B. Nationalizing: Seeing one's own country as the recipient of national promises made by God in the Bible to Israel.

3. Editing God's Mind

A. Embellishing: Reading current thinking into the Bible.

B. Methodologizing: Interpreting the Scripture by means of an unproved theory about the Bible's literary origin.

4. Modernizing the Bible

A. Accommodation: Viewing Scripture through the lens of human reason.

B. Culturalizing: Limiting a text to a specific time in history or culture, when in reality the text demands a wider application in time.

OR

Extending a past practice or culture into our time which in fact should have been limited historically.

5. Twisting Scripture

A. Redefining: Giving historically accepted biblical words new definitions to support our theology.

B. Anglicizing: Reaching inaccurate conclusions by drawing theology from the English text alone.

C. Mysticizing: Finding hidden meanings in Scripture that can be understood only by the one who knows the 'secret code'.

6. Over Literalizing

A. Letterism: Ignoring figures of speech and drawing woodenly literal conclusions.

B. Legalizing: Overemphasizing the letter of God's Word at the expense of its spirit.

7.   Reverse Interpretation

A.   Generalizing: Assuming that any specific historical experience reported in Scripture is a valid, general experience for today.

B.   Experientializing: Reasoning that if any experience has occurred in Scripture, and I have the same experience, then it must be from God, i.e. using experience to validate Scripture instead of vice versa.

8.   Over Systematizing

A.   Dogmatizing: Starting with a conclusion, which is then used to interpret the evidence, thereby assuring that the desired conclusion will be affirmed, i.e. circular reasoning.

B.   Dispensationalizing: Overemphasizing the variations in God's stewardship of redemption throughout history while minimizing God's never-changing dealings with mankind according to His never-changing character.

PART 3

LIVING OUT YOUR CUTS

Fourteen
The Bible's Authority in Your Life

S OMEONE ASKED Charles Spurgeon why he did not defend the Bible against its liberal critics. He responded, 'It's like someone questioning the power of lions. I would not defend a lion to that person; I would simply let the lion out of its cage to defend itself.'

So it is with the Word of God. 'For the word of God is living and active and sharper than any two-edged sword, and piercing as far as the division of soul and spirit, of both joints and marrow, and able to judge the thoughts and intentions of the heart' (Heb. 4:12).

All authority comes from the Word of God – not from men, not from the church, rather from God through His wonderful, righteous Word. We must be willing to submit ourselves to the authority of the Word of God in order to ultimately 'cut it straight'.

Our discussion assumes that God's Word is absolutely authoritative because God is the ultimate Authority.

Thus says the LORD, the King of Israel and his Redeemer, the LORD of hosts: 'I am the first and I am the last, and there is no God besides Me. And who is like Me? Let him proclaim and declare it; yes, let him recount it to Me in order, from the time that I established the ancient nation. And let them declare to them the things that are coming and the events that are going to take place. Do not tremble

and do not be afraid; have I not long since announced it to
you and declared it? And you are My witnesses. Is there
any God besides Me, or is there any other Rock? I know
of none' (Isa. 44:6-8).

We are not developing the doctrine of Scripture's authority
but rather carrying it to its logical conclusion – that since
Scripture is authoritative, then it ought to govern the
conduct of our daily lives.

In order for this to become a dynamic reality, we need to
deliberately commit ourselves to submit to the life-changing
power of the Bible and follow wherever it leads. Four basic
steps of commitment translate right doctrine into the daily
reality of consistent Christian living.

Commitment to receive

First, we are to *receive* the Bible as it is preached, as the
absolute, unswerving, inerrant, infallible Word of God.
Writing to the Thessalonian church, Paul says:

> And for this reason we also constantly thank God that
> when you received from us the word of God's message, you
> accepted it not as the word of men, but for what it really
> is, the word of God, which also performs its work in you
> who believe (1 Thess. 2:13).

Paul knew that he preached not the philosophy of the
day, not the uncertainties of human religious thinkers,
but rather he preached the Word of God, God's eternal
message. It shouted to be accepted as absolute and
everlasting. So the Thessalonians accepted it and received
it for what it was.

Our focus shouldn't be on debating about it, arguing
about it, or questioning it. We need to receive it.

We can reject the Word of God, but that doesn't change its reality. It forever remains the Word of God, and if we in this life refuse to bow the knee and let the Word of God judge our lives, then we later will bow the knee and have our lives judged by God because we rejected Him:

> Therefore also God highly exalted Him, and bestowed on Him the name which is above every name, that at the name of Jesus every knee should bow, of those who are in heaven, and on earth, and under the earth, and that every tongue should confess that Jesus Christ is Lord, to the glory of God the Father (Phil. 2:9-11).

> And I saw a great white throne and Him who sat upon it, from whose presence earth and heaven fled away, and no place was found for them. And I saw the dead, the great and the small standing before the throne, and books were opened; and another book was opened, which is the book of life; and the dead were judged from the things which were written in the books, according to their deeds ... And if anyone's name was not found written in the book of life, he was thrown into the lake of fire (Rev. 20:11-12, 15).

Paul said it best in 2 Timothy 3:16-17: 'All Scripture is inspired by God and profitable for teaching, for reproof, for correction, for training in righteousness; that the man of God may be adequate, equipped for every good work.' That is, all Scripture has been literally breathed out by God so that the book that we revere so dearly and hold so highly is a unique book. It contains the mind and the word and the will of God.

Paul pictures Scripture as a predetermined track on which our lives should run. As long as we stay on the track of right *doctrine*, we travel in the center of God's will. However, because we have the capacity to sin, there are those times when we jump off the track.

The Word of God is not only profitable then to lay out the track for Christian living but also to *reprove* us when we derail. It is possible to travel through life believing we are on course when in fact we have jumped off the track. Scripture serves to warn us that we are off track and need to get back on.

That's where *correction* comes in. The Word tells us how to recover – how to get back on the track. God desires, more than you and I do, that we run on the track. So when we jump off, He has given us the Bible not only to rebuke us lovingly but also to help us return.

Ultimately, God-breathed Scripture profits us by *training in righteousness*. God's Word instructs us how to have fewer accidents as we mature in the Christian faith. As God's Word dwells in us richly (Col. 3:16) we develop better skills in rounding dangerous curves. With time the Word equips us to spend more time on the track than off.

The psalmist says in Psalm 119:89: 'Forever, O Lord, Thy Word is settled in heaven.' Also, the prophet Isaiah writes: 'The grass withers, the flower fades, but the word of our God stands forever' (Isa. 40:8). Aren't you glad there is no need to abandon this Book when a false teacher five years from now proposes that a better book has come along? This is a Book that cannot be improved upon. It is a Book that's forever, non-negotiable, never-changing, and absolute.

A recent television personality had preached for years that wealth is a God-given right and that every person should demand the 'good life' from God. However, during a trip to India she decided that happiness could come through poverty just as well as prosperity. So she has abandoned her

so-called church and television ministry, which ｜
materialism, leaving behind staggering debts.

This true illustration vividly demonstrates that danger
of receiving as authoritative any word other than the Word
of God. Man's word is to be rejected, but God's Word is to
be received as the Thessalonians received it from Paul.

Commitment to feed

Yet 'receiving' the Word is not enough. Many people receive
the Word for what it is. They don't argue whether the Bible
is true or just partially true or half believable. They believe
the Bible is God's Word, but you would not recognize them
as Christians. Why? Because they have failed to make a
second commitment. It is a commitment we find in the life
of Job.

Some may say, 'My life is blessed of God. He's given
me all I could ever ask for – exceeding abundantly above
anything I could ask or think.' Yet there are others who
might use the contemporary phrase, 'I'm in the pits.'

Well, meet Job. He was a man who was 'in the pits'. Life
was dismal and had brought him multiplied disasters. He
says in Job 23:8-9: 'Behold, I go forward but He is not there,
and backward, but I cannot perceive Him. When He acts on
the left, I cannot behold Him; He turns on the right, and I
cannot see Him.' Job was a man who desperately needed to
see God but could not find Him. There were many lights
in Job's life, but one day those lights went out, the shades
came down, and he groped for the reality of God. Yet we
find in verses 10–11 that there was a great confidence in
Job's heart. He says there: 'He [the Lord God] knows the
way I take; when He has tried me, I shall come forth as gold.
My foot has held fast to His path; I have kept His way and

not turned aside.' Here was a man who did not give up on God even when the worst came crashing down.

We ask, 'Why? What was Job's secret?' Job, it seems, had made the commitment in his life not only to *receive* the Word of God but also to *feed* on it. Notice verse 12: 'I have not departed from the command of His lips; I have treasured the words of His mouth more than my necessary food.' That's the diet Job was on. When life crashed in, Job could say, 'Even though I look and don't see, I grope and can't grab hold of, yet I have great confidence in God because I have treasured the words of His mouth more than my necessary food.'

It is sad to see Christians going nowhere, doing nothing, shadow-boxing as it were, and bearing little fruit. I've come to one basic conclusion about such believers: their statement of faith is not necessarily in error, nor have they necessarily abandoned the faith. Rather, feeding on the Word of God is not a personal reality for them. That is why we need to commit ourselves to feed on the Bible. If we're not feeding on the Word of God we'll be without power and we'll be without fruit.

Peter exhorted the early church with these words: 'Therefore, putting aside all malice and all guile and hypocrisy and envy and all slander, like newborn babes, long for the pure milk of the word, that by it you may grow in respect to salvation, if you have tasted the kindness of the Lord' (1 Pet. 2:1-3).

In Amos 8:11 the prophet expresses a fear that is in my own heart, one that I trust never comes true in any of our lives. He says: '... when I will send a famine on the land, not a famine for bread or thirst for water, but rather for hearing the words of the LORD.' I fear that one day there may be a famine in our lives – a lack of daily feeding on the Word of God, that supreme Word, which has been given to nourish our souls, make us healthy, and cause us to grow into what God wants us to be.

The Scripture says man does not live by bread alone but by everything that proceeds out of the mouth of the Lord (Deut. 8:3; Matt. 4:4). I would be like Job, treasuring the Word of God more than my 'necessary food.'

May our souls be satisfied because they have fed on that which is spiritually healthful and worth more than gold and silver. The Word of God is sweeter than honey and gives us hope for things that are future: 'They are more desirable than gold, yes, than much fine gold; sweeter also than honey and the drippings of the honeycomb' (Ps. 19:10).

Commitment to obey

Like the Thessalonians we should receive Scripture, but if that's all we did, we'd fall short of the goal. If we received the Word of God, and if we fed on it daily like Job but stopped at that, we still would miss God's best. We need to make a third commitment.

I love what God has said of Caleb in Numbers 14. The Jews had been liberated from Egypt and were headed for the Promised Land. They were literally just days away from what had been withheld for hundreds of years. Moses sent twelve men into the land. They all viewed the same scenery, they all experienced the same feelings, and they all, in one sense, came back with essentially the same report – there was a tough road ahead. 'Some big people live there, and it doesn't look like we're just going to breeze in and it's ours. It doesn't look like the enemy is just going to blow out of town because we've arrived.'

The majority (ten of twelve) said, 'This is the way the land is. We'd better not take it. We'd better camp right where we are.' But there were two, Joshua and Caleb, who said, 'We agree it's not going to be easy. There are a lot of obstacles to overcome. But we believe we need to penetrate the land because God said He would be with us.'

The contrast from the majority report to that of the minority focuses on Caleb in verse 24. God Himself said, 'But My *servant* Caleb' (emphasis added). How do you become servant of God? Caleb had a different spirit. Here it is – He followed God fully. He was not a 70 percent Christian; he wasn't an 80 percent Christian; he wasn't a 90 percent Christian. He was a 100 percent Christian. He was a man who *fully followed* God. That's what I desire for us – that we would receive the Bible as the Word of God like the Thessalonians, feed on it like Job, who considered it more important than physical food, and then, like Caleb, obey it wholly.

If we don't obey, we may rob ourselves of the full assurance of salvation. Or disobedience could even mean that a person is not God's child at all. The apostle John says there is a direct connection between salvation and obedience to God's Word: 'But whoever keeps His word, in him the love of God has truly been perfected. By this we know that we are in Him: the one who says he abides in Him ought himself to walk in the same manner as He walked' (1 John 2:5-6)

Commitment to honor

I could not conclude without this. In Nehemiah 8, we are spectators to a right response to the Word of God. These people not only received God's Word, they not only fed on it, they not only obeyed it, but they also honored it.

Nehemiah 8:4 says that Ezra the scribe stood at the wooden podium, which they had made for the purpose of reading God's Word. Beside him were a number of others. Ezra opened the book in the sight of all the people, for he was standing above them, and when he opened it they all stood.

It was not a commonplace thing for the Word of God to be opened to these people. It was a sacred time for them, because they opened the book that was holy and which revealed to them the God who was supreme, the God who had called them into a special relationship with Himself. So it was their practice to stand when the Word of God was opened.

Verse 6 says that Ezra then blessed the Lord, the great God, and the people answered, 'Amen, Amen!' Then they bowed low, worshipping the Lord with their faces to the ground. Our response, every time the Word of God is opened, should be worship, for in the pages of the Book are seen the majesty and the greatness of God. There is only one right response to the living God, and that is to bow down and worship Him:

> The twenty-four elders will fall down before Him who sits on the throne, and will worship Him who lives forever and ever, and will cast their crowns before the throne, saying, 'Worthy art Thou, our Lord and our God, to receive glory and honor and power; for Thou didst create all things, and because of Thy will they existed, and were created' (Rev. 4:10-11). .

> And every created thing which is in heaven and on the earth and under the earth and on the sea, and all things in them, I heard saying, 'To Him who sits on the throne, and

to the Lamb, be blessing and honor and glory and dominion
forever and ever.' And the four living creatures kept
saying 'Amen.' And the elders fell down and worshipped
(Rev. 5:13-14).

John Wanamaker, one of America's greatest merchants, once
said: 'I have of course made large purchases of property in
my lifetime ... and the building and grounds in which we are
now meeting represents a value of approximately twenty
billion dollars.

'But it was as a boy in the country, at eleven years of age,
that I made my biggest purchase. In a little mission Sunday
School, I bought from my teacher a small red leather Bible.
The Bible cost me $2.75 – which I paid in small instalments
as I saved. That was my greatest purchase, for that Bible
made me what I am today.'

After that statement, the New York *Herald Tribune*
captioned its write-up thus: 'LATER DEALS IN MILLIONS
CALLED SMALL COMPARED WITH BUYING HOLY
WRIT AT ELEVEN.'

The proclamation of the Word of God, the teaching of
the Word of God, is not to be considered common place,
just something we have heard done all of our lives. That's
profaning the Book and its Author. It is a great privilege
to have the Bible in our hands, to know it and understand
it, to receive it, to feed on it, and obey it. God will hold us
responsible for it. May we be like the Jews in the days of
Ezra, that when the Book is opened, our hearts will bow
down and worship the living God.

The bottom line
I once read a story entitled 'The Diary of a Bible'. It's about a
Bible that recorded its owner's use. One year reads like this:

January 15. Been resting for a week. A few nights after the first of the year my owner opened me but no more. Another New Year's resolution gone wrong.

February 3. Owner picked me up and rushed off to Sunday School.

February 23. Cleaning day. Dusted and put back in my place.

April 2. Busy day. Owner had to present the lesson of the church society meeting. Quickly looked up a lot of references.

May 5. In Grandma's lap again. A comfortable place.

May 9. She let a tear fall on John 14.

May 10. Grandma's gone. Back in my old place.

May 20. Baby born. They wrote his name on one of my pages.

July 1. Packed in a suitcase. Off for vacation.

July 20. Still in the suitcase. Almost everything else taken out.

July 25. Home again. Quite a journey, though I don't see why I went.

August 16. Cleaned again and put in a prominent place. The minister's to be here for dinner.

August 20. Owner wrote Grandma's death in my family record. He left his extra pair of glasses between my pages.

December 31. Owner just found his glasses. Wonder if he'll make any resolutions about me for the new year.

The diary of a Bible. I wonder what my Bible would say if it could write a diary. What would your Bible say if it could write a diary? No doubt none of us would want his Bible's imaginary story published to be read by all.

If my Bible could write, I would want it to say that I had been faithful to live out these four commitments:

1. To receive God's Word like the Thessalonians
'And for this reason we also constantly thank God that
when you received from us the word of God's message, you
accepted it not as the word of men, but for what it really is,
the word of God, which also performs its work in you who
believe' (1 Thess. 2:13).

2. To feed on God's Word like Job
'Behold, I go forward but He is not there, and backward, but
I cannot perceive Him; when He acts on the left, I cannot
behold Him; He turns on the right, I cannot see Him. But
He knows the way I take; when He has tried me, I shall come
forth as gold. My foot has held fast to His path; I have kept
His way and not turned aside. I have not departed from the
command of His lips; I have treasured the words of His
mouth more than my necessary food' (Job 23:8-12).

3. To obey God's Word fully, like Caleb
'But My servant Caleb, because he has had a different spirit
and has followed Me fully, I will bring into the land which
he entered, and his descendants shall take possession of it'
(Num. 14:24).

4. To honour God's Word like Ezra's flock
'And Ezra the scribe stood at a wooden podium which
they had made for the purpose. And beside him stood
Mattithiah, Shema, Anaiah, Uriah, Hilkiah, and Maaseiah
on his right hand; and Pedaiah, Mishael, Malkijah, Hashum,
Hashbaddanah, Zechariah, and Meshullam on his left hand.
And Ezra opened the book in the sight of all the people for
he was standing above all the people; and when he opened it,
all the people stood up. Then Ezra blessed the Lord the great
God. And all the people answered, "Amen, Amen!" while

lifting up their hands; then they bowed low and worshipped the Lord with their faces to the ground.' (Neh. 8:4-6)

When all is said and done, living out these four commitments represents our submission to the authority of God's Word. That's the ultimate in 'cutting it straight'.

Questions for Discussion

1. Read Hebrews 4:12 and Isaiah 44:6-8. What do those passages teach us about the authority of the Word of God?

2. How should we conduct ourselves in view of the authority of Scripture?

3. List the four basic steps of commitment to God's Word. How does each contribute to consistent Christian living?

4. Study 2 Timothy 3:16-17. Describe the ministries the Word provides for us with the help of the ministry of the Holy Spirit.

5. Consider the ways our submission to the authority of Scripture can help us to better 'cut it straight.'

References

1. Jill Morgan, *A Man of the Word: The Life of G. Campbell Morgan* (Grand Rapids: Baker, 1978), pp. 39-40.
2. Roland H. Bainton, *Here I Stand: A Life of Martin Luther* (New York: Mentor Books, 1955), pp. 143-44.
3. *From American Poems,* 3rd. edition (Boston: Houghton, Osgood, 1879), pp. 450-454.
4. Robert Thomas and Stanley Gundry, *Harmony of the Gospels* (Chicago: Moody, 1978), p. 287.
5. D. M. Lloyd-Jones, *Authority,* The Banner of Truth Trust, 1984, p. 35.
6. George W. Peters, *Indonesian Revival* (Grand Rapids: Zondervan, 1973), pp. 80-83.
7. J. Vernon McGee, *Guidelines for the Understanding of the Scriptures* (Pasadena: Thru the Bible Books, n.d.), pp. 3-4.

1	2	3	4
5	6	7	8
9	10	11	12
13	14	15	16

17			
	18		

	19		
20			21
	22		

23			24
25			26

27			
			28

			29
30			

'This book fills a long-awaited need. It makes the Proverbs accessible... a rich resource for every reader.' JOHN MACARTHUR
PRACTICING
PROVERBS
WISE LIVING FOR FOOLISH TIMES
RICHARD MAYHUE

Practicing Proverbs

Wise Living for Foolish Times

Richard Mayhue

This is a unique book on a unique part of Scripture. Mayhue introduces us to Solomon, the writer of Proverbs, and then gets to grips with the book itself and its message. He answers some of the most frequently asked questions about Proverbs and how the book has immediate and pressing relevance to Christians today.

Then, he re-organises the text of the entire book of Proverbs into six life applications – **spiritual, personal, family, intellectual, market-place** and **societal** each also having particular themes highlighted within them.

Practicing Proverbs is one book with multiple uses; devotional, small group discipleship book, resource for the biblical counselor and for teaching Christian ethics and morality.

Most importantly of all, this is a book to help the reader develop a life that glorifies the source of all wisdom – God.

'What a delightful and refreshing spiritual treasury from the pen of Richard Mayhue! The volume is a must for my personal and classroom use and for yours.'

Dorothy Kelley Patterson,
Southwestern Baptist Theological Seminary,

'Dr. Mayhue's book fills a long-awaited need. It makes the Proverbs accessible. This is a marvelous tool for the Bible student, as well as a rich resource for every reader.'

John MacArthur

ISBN 978-1-85792-777-1

FOCUS · ON · THE · BIBLE

1 & 2
THESSALONIANS

TRIUMPHS AND TRIALS
OF A CONSECRATED CHURCH

'He expounds the epistles with impeccable precision.'
William D. Barrick

RICHARD MAYHUE

1 & 2 Thessalonians - Focus on the Bible

Triumphs and Trials of a Consecrated Church

Richard Mayhue

The Thessalonian epistles give us relevant glimpses of the churches earliest times. When looking at the early church many contemporary questions arise such as 'What is true Gospel?' 'How do you plant a church?' These are questions that exercise our modern church just as much as the historic Thessalonian one.

Paul's first letter was written to encourage and reassure the Christians in Thessolonica. He gives thanks for their faith and love; reminds them of his example on godly living and answers questions about the return of Christ. In his second letter we find Paul still dealing with confusion over the return of Christ, especially with those that believed that the Lord's coming had already arrived. He also shows that evil and wickedness will reach a crescendo under the leadership of a mysterious figure called 'the wicked one'. He tells them to remain steady in all that they have learnt.

These timeless letters provide up-to-date answers from a consecrated church, shepherded by godly men devoted to God and to his word.

Mayhue's skill in interpreting the text accurately but with humour and modern parallels comes through in this fascinating commentary.

ISBN 978-1-85792-452-7

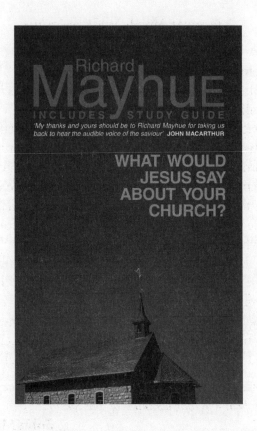

Richard
Mayhue
INCLUDES STUDY GUIDE

'My thanks and yours should be to Richard Mayhue for taking us
back to hear the audible voice of the saviour' JOHN MACARTHUR

WHAT WOULD
JESUS SAY
ABOUT YOUR
CHURCH?

What would Jesus say about your church?

Richard Mayhue

foreword by John MacArthur
Includes study guide

Is your church growing?

The question can be answered in two ways – is it growing numerically or growing spiritually? A church can do the former without the latter, sometimes even the latter without the former! Surely what we want, though, is both.

Richard Mayhue investigates the good and bad points about the churches mentioned in the Bible: The seven churches of Asia, the four Greek churches and the church in Jerusalem. Using the helpful study guide section and questionnaire you can see where your church needs to change.

Many churches today are embarking on an increasingly pragmatic approach 'If it works – then do it!' But in the long term what will 'selling the gospel' do if it replaces evangelism? Richard shows us a clear pathway for us to follow. There is more than enough guidance here to turn the world upside down – just as the early church did!

"My thanks and yours should be to Richard Mayhue for taking us back to hear the audible voice of the Saviour"
John MacArthur

'*If the church is to regain her former glory, it must be through radical transformation by taking the church back to the basics as outlined in Scripture. Mayhue's blend of scholarship with user friendliness makes this book valuable for everyone.*'
Moody Magazine

ISBN 978-1-85792-150-2

Bible Boot Camp

Spiritual Battles in the Bible: and what they can teach you

Richard Mayhue

Today's fast-paced society beguiles us to do what you can get away with. The concept of 'moral fibre' is considered laughable, yet admired in films and yearned for in relationships. How do you develop real moral character? Our TV's say 'send them to Boot Camp!'. Richard Mayhue helps us achieve that spiritually by looking at character building examples in the Bible.

Part one - Warning: some failed to win
Solomon, Jonah, Eve and Saul
Part two - Hope: some fell but recovered while fighting,
Elijah, Samson, Habakkuk and Moses
Part three - Encouragement: some fought to victory,
Joseph, Job, Ruth and Daniel
Part four - Wisdom: gaining God's perspective –
after basic training it's out into the battlefield.

Developing moral courage is important because *what you are* is even more important than *what you know* when you face unforeseen circumstances.

"...for those of you looking to learn how to improve your moral decision making from characters in the Bible"
Christianity Magazine

"Contains a great deal of practical application for this age and culture...recommended for your reading enjoyment and teaching."
Tim LaHaye

978-1-84550-105-1

Richard Mayhue

Foreword by John MacArthur

THE HEALING
PROMISE

Is it always God's will to heal?

Features Joni Eareckson Tada

The Healing Promise

Is it always God's will to heal?

Richard Mayhe

If you need healing, what can you expect from God?

"Jesus brought the healing promise of God but his enemies killed him. Just what that healing gift involves is the subject of this important and encouraging book. You are highly privileged to read this treasure and come away with the richness of God's healing promise."

John MacArthur

God can heal, this is a truth clearly evident from Scripture. We can agree, with absolute certainty, that God still possesses the power to do the miraculous.

But is God using the Faith Healers?

In *The Healing Promise* Richard Mayhue provides straight answers without compromising the Bible or God's miraculous power.

The Healing Promise includes –

A special interview with Joni Eareckson Tada where she talks about coping with the attitudes towards healing she encounters every day

A chapter by André Kole, the man behind many of David Copperfield's illusions, on techniques used in healing meetings.

A special interview with John and Patricia MacArthur about their experiences when Patricia was badly injured in a car accident.

978-1-85792-302-5

Christian Focus Publications
publishes books for all ages

Our mission statement –

STAYING FAITHFUL

In dependence upon God we seek to help make His infallible Word, the Bible, relevant. Our aim is to ensure that the Lord Jesus Christ is presented as the only hope to obtain forgiveness of sin, live a useful life and look forward to heaven with Him.

REACHING OUT

Christ's last command requires us to reach out to our world with His gospel. We seek to help fulfill that by publishing books that point people towards Jesus and help them develop a Christ-like maturity. We aim to equip all levels of readers for life, work, ministry and mission.

Books in our adult range are published in three imprints.

Christian Focus contains popular works including biographies, commentaries, basic doctrine and Christian living. Our children's books are also published in this imprint.

Mentor focuses on books written at a level suitable for Bible College and seminary students, pastors, and other serious readers. The imprint includes commentaries, doctrinal studies, examination of current issues and church history.

Christian Heritage contains classic writings from the past.

Christian Focus Publications Ltd.,
Geanies House, Fearn, Ross-shire,
IV20 1TW, Scotland, United Kingdom
info@christianfocus.com
www.christianfocus.com